A Different Path, A Different Result

A Different Path, A Different Result

A New Consciousness Model for Businesses

By: Cathy A. Archer

iUniverse, Inc.
New York   Bloomington

iUniverse books may be ordered through booksellers or by contacting:

iUniverse
1663 Liberty Drive
Bloomington, IN 47403
www.iuniverse.com
1-800-Authors (1-800-288-4677)

*Because of the dynamic nature of the Internet, any Web addresses or links
contained in this book may have changed since publication and may no longer be
valid. The views expressed in this work are solely those of the author and do not
necessarily reflect the views of the publisher, and the publisher hereby disclaims
any responsibility for them.*

ISBN: 978-1-4401-4593-3 (sc)
ISBN: 978-1-4401-4591-9 (ebook)
ISBN: 978-1-4401-4592-6 (dj)

Printed in the United States of America

iUniverse rev. date: 6/15/2009

Acknowledgement

Thank you Jean Tinder for your new consciousness editing. Your input and insight is most appreciated and your editing is invaluable. Thank you Fred Donathan for taking an image that I love and making it even more perfect. Your creativity comes alive in the book cover. Thanks to all of the people of the Crimson Circle, Geoff, Linda, Norma, Garrett, and staff. And to those of the Crimson Council, thank you for your energetic contribution and guidance, especially Adamus Saint-Germain, I am most grateful and honoured. Thank you Steve Rother of Lightworker for helping me to come out of hiding. I would like to thank my brother James, whose love and support I cannot do without on my projects, my friend Freda for your love and support and review, Mr. D for your continuous love and support over the years, and Conrad for your encouragement. I am especially grateful to my parents and sister for allowing me the space and time to complete this project. And to my daughter Cristin, I am grateful to you for rolling with the punches of the journey that I have taken you on. You are truly an amazing individual and I am honoured to have you on this journey with me. Finally, I would like to thank all of the individuals throughout my life that have helped me to get to where I am. And while there are many who have influenced me along my path, I want to especially thank my graduate Program Director, Dr. Toni Powell, for encouraging me to work in the field of Organization Development, without which this book would not have been possible. Thank you and honour and blessings to you all!

For
my daughter Cristin,
who amazes me with all that she is.

A New Consciousness,
A Different Path,
A New Approach,
A Different Result!

Contents

Introduction.. xiii

Chapter 1:   New Consciousness?...1

Chapter 2:   No More Bosses!..9

Chapter 3:   A System of Interrelated Parts..........................15

Chapter 4:   The Organization...23

Chapter 5:   What's Your Direction?......................................33

Chapter 6:   Operationalize The Strategy.............................39

Chapter 7:   T 'N T — Tools & Training.................................47

Chapter 8:   WIIFM—What's In It For Me?..........................59

Chapter 9:   We Did It!...77

Chapter 10: The Invisible Elephant.....................................83

Chapter 11: No Sticks, Just Carrots!....................................93

Chapter 12: I Hear Your Actions...99

Chapter 13: But, But, But…...109

Chapter 14: Le Résistance...115

Chapter 15: Ready, Set, Go!..119

Introduction

"A journey of a thousand miles begins with a single step."

Lao Tzu (604 BC - 531 BC), The Way of Lao-tzu

For many years, I stood on the sidelines and watched businesses struggle to effectively manage people toward achieving their business goals. In my mind, most attempts always fell short of the mark. It was always obvious to me where managers were going wrong. In my opinion, they never dealt with employees in the right way. I had studied Psychology, Communications, Social Work, had a Master's degree in Human Resources Development, and had some strong views on the people side of things. Then I had a reality check about people and business.

I spent two years working as a manager for a performance-based organization where the focus on performance was so strong that we had telephone conference calls with corporate executives every ten days. There were three days of the month that my colleague and I dreaded. The analysis of our performance occurred on the 11th, the 21st, and the 30th of each month and 'God help us' if our performances were poor. This forced me to be in a constant state of analysis. At the beginning of the month, I had to talk about performances during the previous month. In the middle of the month, I had to talk about how performance for the current month was going and what I had planned to correct any shortfalls for the rest of the month. At the end of the month, I had to forecast performances for the upcoming month.

The most embarrassing part of this entire experience was that I was an HR professional (although not serving in that capacity) who did not have time for any employee issues. When I had extreme HR challenges that had the potential to distract me from the performance focus, I embarrassingly referred the employees to the Human Resources Department. I knew I needed to revamp my eight departments, but I never had time to stop and focus on it. I was already working seven days a week to keep my finger on the pulse of my diverse departments. In addition to dissecting my division challenges, I would also have to dissect the market for our product on a regular basis. I would have to look at the patterns and determine what market segments were responding strongly and which ones weren't. I would then have to identify strategies for attracting more customers from the performing market segments and limit attraction of customers from the non-performing market segments. I finally understood why top executives are paid such big bucks. They are paid for the stress of it all.

One of two things always suffered within my division – either my focus on performance or my focus on people management. What I realized from this experience is that managers do not have the time to be all things to all people. I am extremely appreciative of having had this reality check because it led me to a greater understanding of the challenges faced by managers especially in such a performance-based organization with limited resources and talents.

The other discovery I made while working as an Organization Development Consultant is that many executives still do not realize the value of preventative action in dealing with employees. While I never had the time to set up the right types of structures to address all of my employees' issues, I always found creative ways to make sure they were generally happy. I could not afford for my employees to be unhappy because our performance depended on it! So, I employed various strategies with the people in my division to keep them motivated and performing at maximum capacity.

In my consulting work, I often found myself being called in often when companies were in crises: For instance morale would be very low, employees would be very unhappy, and there would be high turnover, or many union challenges. I always found these situations to be so disconcerting because in almost every situation these occurrences could have been avoided. I know the popular saying, 'hindsight is 20-20.' Nevertheless, I am still always amazed that organizations end up in such crises because they fail to engage in continual analysis and tend to ignore the warning signs.

Both of these types of experiences have led to my unique perspective of what is needed within organizations today. I have developed a business management model that has its foundation in a 'new consciousness' mindset, but represents an integration of some existing strategies. This model meets the needs of executives for bottom line results, while meeting the needs of employees for independence and fulfillment at work. *A Different Path, A Different Result* is not meant to be a scientific discussion, nevertheless its practical application has great value. Implementation of this approach creates a win-win situation for both management and employees. *A Different Path, A Different Result* outlines the philosophy behind the model and guides the reader through a step-by-step explanation of the model. I enthusiastically share my perspective with you, and wish you every success in your endeavors!

Chapter 1:   New Consciousness?

"No one puts new wine into old wineskins. If he does, the wine will burst the skins—and the wine is destroyed, and so are the skins. But new wine is for fresh wineskins."

Jesus Christ, Mark 2:22, New Testament Bible

What is 'new consciousness'? 'Consciousness' denotes awareness. 'New consciousness' suggests a new awareness, which creates a new way of viewing things. This book represents a new approach: A different context within which to view business relations. It is synonymous with 'out of the box thinking'. Executives often talk of this trait, but they rarely exhibit it when it comes to how they view employees.

Band-Aid Please

During my consulting practice, I sometimes ran into brick walls with executives and it was always a most frustrating experience. They would call me into their organizations to help them figure out what was creating the poor organizational climate, but if my findings did not fit into their thinking about organizations and people, they were not readily accepted. Executives traditionally view people from their business perspective, which is usually that concern for the business and concern for employees are mutually exclusive. Thus, they are only interested in what is expedient for their enterprise and this causes them to not want to go beneath the surface and look at the human issues. If the human issues were too bothersome or challenging, they wanted to engage in one of two options: get rid of the 'problem' employees or ignore the problem.

In one organization that I worked with, which was undergoing major changes, an executive voiced a widespread view of frustration about employee issues. After I described the state of affairs within his organization and explained how it is common for employees undergoing such a change to develop a sense of confusion and distrust, especially if executives aren't communicating enough about the changes, he responded, "We should fire the lot of them and start over." In the minds of executives, many of employees' perceptions and reactions within organizations are illogical. Dealing with human emotion and organizational dynamics can be confusing to business executives and many of them don't want to address emotional issues. In the minds of most business executives, humanness is to be left outside the front door.

It became clear to me in my consulting work that some business executives were not really interested in resolving their organizational challenges. They simply wanted to put a 'band-aid' on any organizational issues that threatened productivity. They wanted to fix the problem to the extent that it allowed business to go on as usual. Anything beyond that was too much to ask for. So I asked myself, how can I get executives to meet the needs of their employees while meeting their own needs as well? I knew I had to find a way to do both and in doing so, I identified essential elements that could not be ignored and will be revealed throughout this book. The first basic requirement is that businesses have to be restructured to become *people focused.*

Employees Are Human

It may seem obvious, but all too often it appears that executives forget their employees are still human, and cannot help but to bring their humanness to work each day. Their humanness cannot be ignored. It has always been my contention that the employees' state of being is the determining factor in the success of any organization. Therefore, my organizational assessments within companies always went beyond the surface to assess the human side of the challenges.

When I first discovered my ability to assess organizations at such a depth, I was excited by it. After my graduate school professor lauded me for my unique ability to be thorough and comprehensive in assessing an organization's culture, I thought of this skill as a gift and enthusiastically began to put it to work. But the more I tried to put this into practice, the more frustrated I became. Nevertheless, I still felt the 'human' issue was central to an organization's effectiveness.

We have to accept that employees bring this humanness to work with them daily. This is an important factor in any effective management approach, and the basis for the approach outlined in this book. There are many theories on understanding employees within organizations and even more on management styles based on the 'humanness factor.' However, my difficulty with many of them is that they don't go far enough in what they propose within organizations.

There are two essential elements missing from the various practices that actually do consider the humanness factor. The first is the lack of consideration of the existing frameworks or boxes within the minds of executives. Executives' practices in thinking create limitations in the way they address the humanness factor—their philosophical thinking about employees and business limits the effectiveness of existing human relations management approaches. The second missing element is the lack of consideration and integration of all of the interrelated systems impacting both the people needs and business needs dynamics. In other words, every aspect of an organization is interrelated with every other aspect, and together they determine an organization's effectiveness. While the human factor is acknowledged and promoted by many Social Scientists and Theorists, it is my contention that many of these current practices represent 'new wine in old wine skins' – new practices within an old mindset.

New Wine in New Wine Skins

In adopting any management style, one must begin with one's philosophical approach to organizations and employee management. This determines the effectiveness, or the lack thereof, of any management model. Adopting a Human Relations Theory of management, for example, would not work effectively if your basic premise or belief is that employees are simply there to serve your purpose of achieving your task objectives and are thus seen as a means to an end, rather than people with human needs. (The Human Relations Theory of management is based on the individual's desire for self-actualization and focuses on fulfilling the needs of organization members.[1]) 'Pseudo adoption' of the Human Relations Theory style of management is demonstrated in those organizations where they have what is considered progressive employee development and other programs, but they still possess an opposing undercurrent that reveals a lack of real value for their employees and their needs. What executives do not realize is that employees already perceive what is a real value and what is not, and therefore such programs do not always serve the purpose for which they were intended, which is to demonstrate that executives value employees.

---

1   Discussions on Human Relations theory can be found in *Organizational Communication* by G.L. Kreps. (1990) Longman. White Plains, N.Y.

Then, the executives do not understand why the organizational challenges continue, and thus view employees as ungrateful and unappreciative of management's efforts. The bottom line is that progressive employee development programs cannot exist within a vacuum. Their effectiveness, or the lack there of, is impacted by other organizational dynamics.

This is at issue within a number of companies. I discovered one prime example in a large organization, which frequently demonstrated their lack of real value for their employees. When I conducted assessments with the employees, every single employee interviewed revealed that the benefits the company offered were quite good. (This company had a reputation for having great compensation packages and was considered to be one of the best paid in the city.) It offered good salaries, health insurance, a very good retirement package, education reimbursement, lots of training programs, etc. As a matter of fact, this was one of the few times I had encountered employees who were so pleased with the company benefits. Yet, morale was low and there was a high level of distrust toward management.

The organizational dynamics were revealing. A number of employees were sometimes treated unfairly, which created a poor organizational climate. The way the company's training programs were administrated is one example. The company had a large budget for out-of-town training programs. In one division in particular, the perception among many of the employees was that managers always chose favored employees to attend out-of-town training. And in some instances, the same employees were chosen several times. Even the recipients of the training opportunities admitted during interviews that there was no logic behind the methods for choosing individuals to attend training, and that some individuals seemed to be continuously passed over. Unfortunately, this also extended to promotion opportunities and bonuses. Many of the decisions made were more a function of management's preferences as opposed to company policy. And while there were good company policies in place, employees often focused upon and outlined the many exceptions made contrary to company policy.

The amazing thing was that more than one manager engaged in many of these unfair practices. This organization clearly had a culture of authoritarian practices that worked against its employee programs, which defeated its attempts to show its progressiveness in employee development.

The philosophical approach of managers in this instance was clearly not conducive to its stated values. Any values that a company wishes to espouse have to be fully and widely demonstrated to have any real effect. In many instances, companies engage in games of pretense and thus reap no benefits from their efforts to meet the needs of and communicate the value of their employees. Organizations wishing to be progressive in their treatment of employees must embrace a new way of thinking about them and their roles in the organization in order for progressive programs to really serve its purpose.

A Different Path, A Different Result presents a new consciousness approach to organizational practices. It discusses a new philosophy and perspective from which to view organizations. It proposes a new model that remains true to its basic philosophy, and while some of the components of the model are not entirely new, the overall approach and the interrelatedness of its components do represent a new way of thinking. *A Different Path, A Different Result* takes various existing and forward-thinking theories or premises of human behavior (although this book will not include detailed theoretical discussions) and places them within 'new wineskins' to ensure the effectiveness of a management style that takes the humanness factor into consideration. This new model has the core objective of creating a win-win situation for both executives and employees in their attempts to achieve organizational objectives. It contends that business objectives and employee goals can be mutually inclusive and compatible, and its basic philosophy is described in the chapters that follow.

Chapter 2:   No More Bosses!

"When you always do what you have always done, you will always get what you have always gotten."

Anonymous

We live in a society in which we pretend to believe that all men are created equal. Yet, our society is fraught with demonstrations to the contrary. All aspects of society reflect who we really are and what we really believe. In business, for example, the bosses are seen as mini gods whom we must not offend. They wield their power and control the minions with a threat of their signature on dreaded forms. Productivity is sought through coercion in most instances. Creativity is discouraged. Minions are to be kept in their place. And while this is not the norm in every single business, in a twenty-first century world, it represents far too many businesses. We need a new approach to business—we need to take a different path in order to realize a different result!

This model has a precondition of businesses becoming more people focused, which, to reiterate, is not mutually exclusive to having a business focus. Becoming people focused begins with the eradication of all bosses. The idea of 'no more bosses' may make executives indignant at first thought. Nonetheless, its import is quite acceptable. The concept of 'no more bosses' quite simply means removing the sense that there is a difference between executives, or managers, and employees. It suggests getting rid of the 'I am more important than you' thinking of managers, and the perceived or real elevated status of executives. This concept is not new to the business world and its practice is even attempted within some organizations, but to what avail? In actuality, its current practices bear lip service to the concept at best, in most cases. Organizations hold this concept of 'each employee is important' as "espoused theory"[2] but it is not fully demonstrated within organizations, or, it is not a "theory-in-use."[3] Once again, it is new wine in old wine skins.

As human beings, there are no differences among individuals in terms of importance on planet Earth. It is widely accepted that each individual human's life is equal in value to any and every other human's life, in theory at least. In practice, however, there are many indications that this value is once again more 'espoused theory' rather than 'theory-in-use.' By the mere choices that are made, our biases towards some individuals reveal themselves. Our societal norms often dictate these biases and enshrine them in our every behavior. For example, you don't ever hear parents extolling the virtues of being a garbage collector, or even a filing clerk, yet these are necessary occupations for our society to survive. Demonstrations of these biases pervade our society on many levels, and it can be clearly seen within organizations. When have you ever heard of the janitor, or even the mail clerk, within an organization receiving kudos or recognition for their work efforts at the same level

---

2   Discussions on espoused theory in the organizational context can be found in *Knowledge for Action: A Guide to Overcoming Barriers to Organizational Change.* Chris Argyris (1993) Jossey-Bass, San Francisco, CA
3   Discussions on the concept of theory-in-use can be found in *Knowledge for Action: A Guide to Overcoming Barriers to Organizational Change.* Chris Argyris (1993) Jossey-Bass, San Francisco, CA

as the organization's top performing salesman? Still, many executives pretend to believe that their organizations exhibit the value that all of their employees are considered important or equal.

The approach outlined in this book does not pretend to offer corrections for society's inappropriate dictates, nor can it cure the ills of the world as a whole. It attempts to reveal the inadequacies in our current consciousness thinking within organizations and offers a new method for achieving one's organizational goals that allows such values as 'everyone is important' to become real values, or, values-in-use.

Walk In My Shoes

This new perspective involves re-thinking business relationships and business operations. It begins with a new view of each individual involved in your business operations, which is that *each individual has to be viewed as you*. Whenever you look at an individual, you have to see yourself. It is similar to 'walking in another's shoes.' When you can see each individual as yourself, suddenly their views, their feelings, their aspirations, and their challenges become your views, your feelings, your aspirations, and your challenges. In other words, all that is important to them becomes important to you.

It is not so much about feeling their pain and solving their challenges for them. Viewing each individual as yourself allows you to respect them as individuals, and value their goals for their lives as much as you value your own. When you begin with this premise that each individual involved in your business deserves just as much respect as you do, then each act within which you become engaged will be in their best interest as well as your own.

The core suggestion is that executives and managers must truly come to believe that the feelings, thoughts, desires and goals of employees are just as important as their own. This then becomes the basis upon which all decisions and actions within the organization occur. I am sure you are familiar with the saying, 'when you always do what you have always done, you will always get what you have always gotten.' This is powerfully true. If you want different results within your organization, you have to be prepared to try a different approach.

So, the premise of this approach is that each and every individual within an organization has thinking, feelings, and goals that are equally important, including the chief executive's. And no individual's goals and objectives have to be mutually exclusive to the organization's goals and objectives. This is the foundation of the philosophy of this new consciousness business model.

Anarchy Afoot?

In the minds of many executives the first thought is, "how much will this cost?" For whatever reasons, they tend to believe that caring about employees beyond a superficial level will cost them dearly. Not necessarily. At least not in dollars and cents, but it could cost in terms of initial time and energy invested in the implementation of this model. However, I contend that you will discover over time that it is worth every bit of the time and effort spent.

Another thought might be that within such an organization using this approach, there will be total anarchy. No. The idea of 'no boss' or 'everyone being equal' speaks more to the perspective from which to view each employee. It is more about the lack of a boss, than it is about the lack of a leader and there is a difference. A boss is viewed far differently than a leader. When you say the word 'boss' to an employee, and you say the word 'leader' to that employee, it conjures up two completely different images in their perception. So the idea of getting rid of the bosses is more about getting rid of the implications inherent in the term. It really is about changing the roles of these individuals. This philosophy advocates removing the concept of 'the boss' and replacing it with the concept of 'leadership' and 'self-leadership.' This approach of leadership will be expounded upon in subsequent chapters.

This philosophy is founded in the belief that each individual is a powerful, self-determining individual with life choices and decision-making authority. And it requires true acceptance of each individual as such, thus going beyond being an espoused theory and becoming a 'theory-in-use.' It presupposes no judgment of the individual choices made but simply proposes to encourage each individual to be the best that they can be in their chosen roles. If it is garbage collection or banking, it offers the same support and structures to allow the individual to be the best garbage collector or banker that they can be. With every decision and at every juncture, the core premise is to always create a win-win situation for all.

Chapter 3:   A System of Interrelated Parts

"Everything affects everything else in one way or another. Whether you are aware of that or not does not change the fact that this is what is happening. That's why I say a business is a system. This systems perspective reminds us that this is what is going on. And when you see it this way, you can manage your business better. You appreciate, for example, that any action will reverberate throughout the entire company. This causes you to pay more attention to what you do, and learn the right lessons from your experience."

John Woods[4]
Work in Progress

Every aspect of every organization is interrelated and each aspect impacts overall performance. Therefore, it is not enough to simply adopt a new view of employees and then continue with business as usual. All of the elements within an organization have to be aligned with the new perspective to produce the desired results, thus requiring a systematic approach to ensure effective individual and organizational performance.

---

4   *Quote Source: http://www.worldtrans.org/whole/wsquotes.html*

There are several internal factors that must be assessed to ensure alignment with the organizational objectives. This model requires systematic reviews to ensure not only that the human elements are aligned but that the non-human elements are as well. The problem is that many company executives tackle problems in isolation, with little or no consideration of how they relate to and impact various aspects of the organization.

A particular organization that I worked with was experiencing a problem with a machine that produced large volumes of invoices. Because of this problem, individuals in the billing department had to manually prepare invoices until management could get the machine fixed. It turned out that the machine could not be fixed and a new one needed to be ordered. The person responsible for addressing the challenge was so far removed from operations that he seemed to be in no hurry to resolve the situation, which produced a cascade effect of problems. In the ensuing months, the staff in the billing department could not get statements out in a timely manner; because customers were not receiving their bills, some were not meeting the payment deadlines; the disconnect department got overloaded with disconnects; and the credit and collections department got overloaded with collection files. This domino effect had a major impact on revenue collections for several months because no one seemed to realize how one challenge was impacting the entire organization.

Every organization must be viewed as one system with interrelated parts: The human element, the systems, the structures, and the processes are all interrelated. An effective leader has to make certain that the right structures, processes, and systems are in place, along with a conducive work culture, and that all are working together effectively so that the employees' ability to be successful is not hampered and organizational objectives can be achieved.

Ducks In A Row

Organizational effectiveness goes beyond the realization of the interrelatedness of the various organizational components. Each component has to be aligned. When planning within the organization, executives decide on the strategic goals and objectives, and then a plan is created for achievement of the goals. The level of success in achieving strategic goals will be determined by one thing: organizational alignment. Success will be limited unless every aspect of the organization is working congruently to achieve organizational objectives. (*See the diagram1 for alignment components.*)

Diagram 1

<u>ALIGNMENT OF ORGANIZATIONAL COMPONENTS</u>

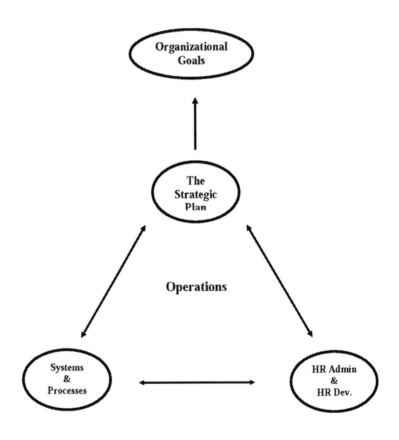

The organization is made up of several components that are essential to functioning. These include the Strategic Plan, Human Resources (HR), and Systems & Processes. These components must be in alignment to achieve the highest levels of success for the organization. It is especially so with this model. Without the various components working congruently, the ability to see unprecedented results from a new consciousness approach is jeopardized.

The HR component includes human resources administration and human resources development. Separate and apart from the HR philosophy, the administration function of selection must align with the needs identified in the Strategic Plan. For example, if the goals that the organization are trying to reach require very detail-oriented individuals in a particular department, and that department has a need for a staff increase, then HR must ensure that this skill (detail-oriented) is present in the individuals hired during the selection process. Not ensuring that new hires are detail-oriented immediately puts the achievement of the strategic objectives and the organizational goals at risk. Additionally, the employee benefits and policies must be conducive to the organizational strategies identified in the Plan. Concomitantly, the training and development of employees must be aimed at meeting the needs dictated by the Strategic Plan, as should succession planning. All aspects of HR must be examined to ensure alignment with the Strategic Plan in addition to this philosophical approach.

The Systems & Processes also need to align with the strategies and the HR component. The chosen systems and processes for goal achievement need to be efficient and effective for maximizing the level of success. The level of success can be determined by how conducive the systems and processes are to the employees engaged in their use. For example, if one of your strategic objectives is to decrease the delivery time on products sent to customers in order to improve on company image, you can clearly see how the components would need to line up to meet this goal. Employees involved in each step of the process would have to be committed to working efficiently and effectively to decrease their processing time; systems would have to be running efficiently; and processes would have to make sense and be structured in a way that would decrease the delivery timeframe.

To take the example further, if the process involves inputting orders into a computer system before sending them to the warehouse for fulfillment, and one employee's system works slowly while the other computers work at maximum speed, that one system affects the ability of the entire department to decrease delivery time. The steps of each process would also have to be examined to ensure that the processes used are the most logical and effective for achieving the objective of decreasing delivery timeframes.

It is critical to remember that all aspects of the organization have to be in alignment with each other as well as congruent with the philosophy inherent in this approach.

Just as all components of the organization are interrelated and work together, all of the individuals within the organization are interrelated and must cooperate to produce the desired results. Creating a win-win situation means creating a partnership and getting both parties—executives and employees—happily working toward the same goals. It isn't as much a focus on being a team as much as it is a focus on the understanding of the underlying connectivity of everyone's goals. In other words, it requires an acceptance of the premise that 'in order for me to achieve my goals, you have to be able to achieve yours.' Additionally, executives must be committed to ensuring that employees are given every opportunity to succeed.

Since both organizational objectives and employee objectives are mutually inclusive, achieving both sets of objectives requires executives to buy-in to employees' individual objectives, and employees to buy-in to organizational objectives. It is imperative because it is very difficult to achieve any success without the agreement, support, and cooperation of those involved. This new consciousness model features a major focus on both the company goals and the employee's individual goals and self-development plans, thus respecting the partnership and ensuring that goal achievement is a two-way street.

The Essentials

This new consciousness model is laid out in two major parts. The first outlines steps toward achievement of the organizational goals in keeping with the model's philosophy; and the second outlines the approach for assisting employees with the achievement of their own goals, also in keeping with this model's philosophy. The second element represents the materialization of this philosophical approach and is vital to the effectiveness of this model. Therefore, implementing this approach mandates that executives make an internal commitment to change their perspective and fully adopt the philosophy of an approach of partnership. Then they can begin creating employee buy-in and commitment to the organization's goals and consequently, realization of the desired results.

Here are the essential viewpoints or perspectives that have been synthesized for this new consciousness mindset:

1. Every employee and business associate's goal is just as important as those of the executives, therefore employees and executives should form a partnership with the core purpose of helping each other to achieve their goals;
2. The organization consists of a system of interrelated parts that impact upon each other, therefore the creation of every organizational component and the execution of every action must be considered in the context of its rippling effect;
3. There is an underlying connectivity of everyone's

goals. No individual within the partnership can reach their goal without the other, therefore it behooves both partners to work together to help and support each other, and in so doing both partners can reach their individual goals.

These create the foundation upon which every action is built and together they form the philosophy of this new consciousness business model.

It is important to understand that this model cannot be approached in an 'a la carte' fashion. One cannot choose to adopt bits and pieces and expect it to be effective. Its philosophical premise must be accepted as a coherent whole, and it must be approached as a system of interrelated parts to be effective in its implementation.

Chapter 4:   The Organization

"I spent months and months asking myself, "What is an organization?" If I'm talking about institutional and organizational change, what am I really talking about? What is an organization in the deepest sense? It surely isn't just a set of bylaws, because I can write a set of bylaws and shove it in a desk drawer, and it just becomes an old moldering piece of paper. And if you really think deeply about it, you discover that every organization and every institution, without exception, has no reality save in your mind. It's not its buildings. Those are manifestations of it. It's not its name, it's not its logo, and it's not some fictional piece of paper called a stock certificate. It's not money. It is a mental concept around which people and resources gather in pursuit of common purpose."

Dee Hock[5]

If an organization is based on "a mental concept," one can assume that the organization can be developed to fit one's desires. One can create the right structures, processes, and the right organizational culture that are most conducive for achieving the goals. It appears that many executives feel stuck

---

5   *Quote Source: WIE: Business Transformation Through Chaos Theory: http://www.wie.org/j22/hock.asp*

with whatever structures, processes, and culture they already have because it seems very little is done to address those aspects of their organizations that are ineffective.

"It Has Always Been Done This Way"

If you did a survey in any number of organizations and you asked the question, "Why do you use this process or system of doing things?" you will often hear employees and managers alike respond either, "I don't know," or "We have always done it this way." I'll bet that there will only be a small percentage that will give you logical reasons for their processes.

In many businesses today, practices are adopted and maintained because people often tend to accept things as they are. Many organizational structures, performance review systems, organizational processes, etc. are a result of adopting the position of 'this is the way it has always been done.' The unfortunate thing about this practice is that common sense or logic is sacrificed in order to maintain the status quo. The opposite is not necessarily the best thing either, which is adopting every new business fad that comes on the market because it is 'fashionable.' That is another mistake.

All processes, systems and structures that are created or chosen should be ones that can bring about the best results. All aspects of an organization must be made conducive to the overall direction, otherwise the organizational components are working against the organization itself. Every decision ever made within your organization, every adoption of a new practice should be based on what serves your business best.

Who's On Top?

There should be no such thing as a 'standard organizational structure,' although most businesses choose a top down organizational structure because it is the most common.

However, every organizational structure sends a message. What message is yours sending? Is your structure one that is focused on status preservation? Is it one that is focused on bottom line results? Is it one that is focused on employee independence? Alignment with this new consciousness model requires an organizational structure to have a focus on both partners achieving their objectives. Thus, the best organizational structure is one that is aligned with the philosophy of creating a win-win situation for both executives and employees, and it must communicate the core values inherent in this philosophy. It must be reflective of a leadership perspective as opposed to a boss perspective. It must be reflective of a partnership and engender self-leadership. And it must have a focus on goal achievement for both partners. If your organizational structure is aligned with this philosophy, then meeting both sets of (partners') goals is more likely.

"But, I Am The Boss!"

If an organization has a structure that has a strong focus on a top down hierarchy, it can send the message that status is the core value, which can promote a 'boss mentality.' If a culture is reflective of a boss mentality as opposed to a leadership mentality, it can negatively impact the organizational climate. There are inherent problems in creating a culture of 'I am the boss.' It elicits a specific response because there is a specific attitude that is communicated with this position. That attitude is,

> "I am the boss and you are not!"
> "I am in charge and you are not!"
> "You must listen to me, but I don't have to listen to you!"
> "You must do as I say—no questions asked!"

This is how 'I am the boss' is interpreted, which can induce specific and detrimental responses. I saw this firsthand with one of my clients. I was conducting assessments with the staff of my client, whose organization was experiencing morale challenges and a very poor organizational climate. Their organizational structure was one that had a traditional hierarchy and a culture that was very focused on 'boss status.' One of the things that I discovered was staff members who were very competent and responsible in their thinking about their work tasks, yet these attributes were not fully manifested. I was amazed at the high level of competence that was prevalent among the different departments, because I had been led by executives to believe otherwise. However, the work culture was such that the idea of being a boss was so important that management seemed to have lost sight of their purpose of 'reaching the organization's goals.' Their focus seemed to be more about maintaining their status as opposed to delivering results.

The employees within this organization communicated specific challenges to me that they were faced with which hampered productivity. However, they were always able to communicate what was required to resolve the challenges. When asked whether or not these resolutions were discussed with their managers, they had one of three responses: 1. "They are the boss, so they should know how to fix the problem." 2. "They didn't ask, so I didn't tell them anything." 3. "Yes, but nothing was ever done."

If a manager is busy asserting her (*for ease of reference)* position as a boss, it is counter intuitive for her to look to an employee for answers. If who she is at work is based on her view of herself as the boss, she can't appear to listen to the views of her employees. This view of herself can cause her to be dismissive of employees' viewpoints and insights and can prove counter productive as in the example just cited, as well as the one that follows.

You Have To Crawl Before You Can Walk!

A number of years ago I was told this story by a young lady named Ari. She worked as an Assistant Training Coordinator for a government run training center. One of her responsibilities was to place the trainees within businesses for on-the-job training. During her first year, she made calls to many businesses to request their participation in the job-training program and was amazed to discover that many of them did not wish to participate. "Who wouldn't want a worker for free?" she thought. Well, they didn't, and they all had the same reason—while the students had good technical skills, their attitudes left a lot to be desired.

For a bachelor level Psychology graduate this was a grand opportunity to fix the problem. So, she began by conducting research. She chose to interview a random sample of students from a group of students that ended up before the administration on behavioral issues, although, they had no idea they were chosen from such a group. She asked them questions about the behavior of their peers because it is always easier to talk about why others are behaving the way they are. But in truth the information is more a reflection of the individual's own thinking, which of course was what she really wanted. The results were interesting and led her to develop a program for students that focused on building self esteem, goal setting, decision making, developing positive attitudes etc.

In Ari's mind, this program was perfect. It had lots of group discussions and exercises, and was designed to have lasting impact. Ari excitedly submitted her program proposal to the General Manager for approval. The proposal explained the rationale, the method she used for research, the outline for each class etc. A few days later when Ari went to follow up with the General Manager, she was given a lecture. In the middle of the lecture, the Manager uttered the words, "You have to crawl before you could walk." She could not have been more disappointed, but she got the message loud and clear. "You are a minion, and you are not supposed to have a good idea." The General Manager clearly demonstrated that she was the boss and wanted no part of Ari's new idea.

You may wonder if the manager was right and Ari's program may not have been a good one. Ari found out later that a manager running a campus in another location got a copy of the program, implemented it, and saw stunning results. Apparently, the word around that campus among students was that 'it's the class to take,' and the students not signed up for the program would often ask when would it be placed on their schedule. And, most importantly, in later years businesses reported an improvement in the attitudes of students they received for job training who had participated in this program.

It appears that not much has changed in the 21st century. Having coffee with a friend one day, the server surprisingly vented his frustrations about how 'the bosses' do not listen to the employees and do not accept their suggestions. This was in response to a few suggestions my friend had made to the employee about the business. Unfortunately, I have found this to be a common sentiment expressed by employees of my clients.

The most regrettable thing is that many individuals buy into the idea that the bosses are the ones with the good ideas. In some cases, employees that have good ideas don't express them; or they do express them and have frustrating experiences as a result. Many employees don't even bother to think of any new ideas because they understand the pecking order. Organizations are disadvantaged as a result of this 'boss mentality' because innovative ideas can increase a company's bottom line. Every time an employee's idea is not heard, companies risk losing the potential to increase the bottom line.

Follow The Leader

The idea of 'bosses' is not congruent to an effective organization and is certainly not congruent with this new consciousness model. It has to be about leadership. True leaders are seen as role models. True leaders engender followers. True leaders invite participation. True leaders <u>inspire</u> followers to deliver on results.

The structure that is most advocated for this model is one that engenders leadership and allows for the creation of self-leadership. Self-leadership can evolve from a practice of leadership, as leaders are emulated. Self-leadership is more conducive to a partnership. Self-leadership engenders individual responsibility, which leads to individual accountability and increased productivity. All aspects of this model focus on creating a culture of individual responsibility and accountability thus creating self-leadership. Creating an environment that encourages self-leadership is more likely to help achieve organizational objectives than the traditional work environments.

Your Organization's Culture

Whatever message is communicated by your organizational structure also influences your organization's culture (*See chapter 10 for more on organizational culture*). Work cultures are not made up of rules that are written down, but evolve from the organizational practices and behavior of its members. The work culture is a representation of the organization's values and interpretations of how things work within the organization. And, because the organization's culture consists of commonly understood behaviors and is shaped by employee perceptions, executives have to ensure that they are not sending the wrong messages.

Wrong messages are any messages not intended to be

sent. Inadvertent messages are a common occurrence in many organizations and can end up with disastrous results. The most disturbing thing is that many executives and managers are not even aware that these messages are being sent, as revealed in the following example.

I was asked to conduct an organizational assessment of a company because the training manager suspected the organization was missing out on opportunities for increased revenue, and she wanted to know if this was in fact happening and why. The main challenge that I discovered, that in fact created missed opportunities for revenue collection, was the fact that the company grew in size so quickly that it didn't take time for self-analysis of its processes and procedures, nor did it take time to ensure that each department was aware of what the new departments were doing. So, if potential clients called the company for information, they were sometimes told that the company didn't offer particular services, which the company did in fact offer.

However, the most startling discovery of missed opportunities for increased revenue was that members of one department intentionally told their existing clients that their company did not offer particular services that were in fact offered by other departments. There were approximately three departments affected by this practice. During employee interviews, it was suggested to me that individuals with the most contacts were promoted. In other words, if you had more clients that were specific to you and you were able to get them to purchase products from you, you were favored among management for promotion. And while this wasn't a specific policy, it was a practice that was understood by all. So, if I can get a promotion because I have rich clients that no one else shares, why would I share them with another department? If I say to my client, "yes we do offer that product," it means that I would have to pass that client on to another department. So naturally I would rather my client purchase that product from another company than share him/her with a colleague and possibly lose an opportunity for promotion.

In the company's attempt to reward high performers, it decreased its opportunities for revenue generation and the entire organizational culture created a counter productive work environment. In addition to creating counter productive results with its earnings, it had created such a competitive environment that knowledge sharing was also inadvertently discouraged. If an individual discovered a specific problem solving method that increased his performance, he did not share that with his colleagues because being a problem solver was also lauded. This organization's practices sent the wrong messages, which created an organizational culture that resulted in counter productive measures and results. While these practices in and of themselves are not bad, you have to ensure that organizational practices are not sending the wrong messages and are therefore counter productive.

Remember, everything affects everything within your organization. Therefore, you must ensure that your organizational structure and practices are congruent with both this philosophical approach and with the strategies for goal achievement.

Chapter 5: What's Your Direction?

"If you cry "Forward!" you must without fail make plain in what direction to go. Don't you see that if, without doing so, you call out the word to both a monk and revolutionary, they will go in directions precisely opposite?"

Anton Chekhov[6]
Russian dramatist & short story author (1860 - 1904)

The systematic approach that is required for implementation of this new consciousness model consists of a series of interrelated steps involving the various organizational components. It begins with first of all understanding your goal. What is it that you ultimately want to achieve? What direction do you wish to take the organization, and how do you propose to get there? It is imperative that you identify the goals for your organization. It doesn't necessarily have to be a part of a grand strategic plan. However, I would recommend that some kind of formal planning process take place that outlines what you are trying to accomplish with your organization. Otherwise, you run the

---

6   *Quote Source: http://www.greatest-quotations.com/search.asp?quote=revolutionary*

risk of being a directionless ship upon which all else is based. Imagine the consequences of your efforts on a ship without direction!

The CEO needs to identify the specific business goals on which he wishes to focus. These could be several goals related to various departments. It does not matter. The bottom line is that specific goals need to be identified toward which everyone can focus.

Once you know the direction in which you wish to head, you must have a plan to get there. A popular goal that many executives like to set for their organizations is to reduce cost by a certain percentage within the next fiscal year. The mistake that many executives make with a goal like this is that they communicate it to the employees in a general sense and possibly throw out a few suggestions on how this can be done organization wide. But often there are no specific strategies or plans of action beyond their product cost reduction strategies, and sometimes not even then. It is absolutely necessary to create a process to ensure that you have the right strategies and a plan of action to make all of your goals happen.

Everybody, Somebody, Anybody, and Nobody

If you want organization-wide cost reduction along with product cost reduction, leaving it to happenstance is not going to ensure you reaching your goal. Think about it. In your company, who takes responsibility for getting something done when it isn't assigned to a specific person or department? If everyone isn't assigned a specific role in making this happen, no one will take responsibility to ensure it happens. Remember the story about Everybody, Somebody, Anybody and Nobody? "Everybody was asked to do an important job. Even though it was Everybody's job, Everybody thought Somebody would do it. Everybody didn't realize that Nobody would do it. Anybody could have done it, but Nobody did it. And Everybody blamed

Somebody." (*Anonymous*) Also, if people aren't told how, or given a plan of action or a path to get there, it is not likely to happen either.

Therefore, you must determine the direction on which everyone will focus, identify the strategies that will be used, and create a plan of action that will get you there. Given world economic affairs at this time, many businesses are probably focused on tightening their belts while still maintaining profits. So, for illustration purposes we will create a company and use a goal to which most businesses can relate:

COMPANY: **New Energy Enterprises**

GOAL: Reduce operational costs in 2009 by 20%.

A 20% cost reduction has been identified as the main goal. Several goals can be simultaneously worked toward, however only one will be used for illustration purposes.

This process begins by identifying specific goals for each department. In other words, the goal of 'reducing costs by 20% for the company overall' needs to be split among the various departments. For example, the accounts department could be charged with the responsibility of reducing the company's costs overall by 10%, while other departments could have smaller goals that could be reached by finding ways to cut down on the cost of supplies by more efficient use of them, or practicing better maintenance habits on office machines to reduce repair costs etc.

The key is to ensure that each department has specific targets that contribute to the achievement of the overall goal of reducing costs by 20%. However, it does not end with just communication of the department's goal. A plan of action will need to be outlined for each department and created along with the department personnel. Once the goal is established and targets identified for each department, it is time to communicate the vision.

Communicate The Vision

In order to get anyone to agree to, or work toward, a particular set of goals or direction, that individual needs to understand what the goals are or what the direction is. I often use an example given to me by an employee of a past client to illustrate the importance of this point. He complained that his management had not shared the new direction of the company with the staff. He said, "It's like all of the employees getting into a row boat and being told to row, but we are not told where we are going. How do we row if we don't know where we are going? The company could be aiming for Florida, and we end up arriving in New York because the employees do not know where we are supposed to be heading!"

Employees have to be told where the company is trying to go. What is the organization's vision? What are you trying to accomplish? What impact would you like your organization to have? How important are your goals? In other words, why should we (employees) care? And just as important as 'the sharing' of the vision, is *how* the vision is shared. It must be communicated with passion and conviction. A picture must be painted of the organization and employees drawn into its beauty. Creating an emotional connection with employees during the delivery of the message is essential to the buy-in process. Without getting into a detailed discussion, it's suffice to note that research reveals that emotions play an important role in influencing individuals in any direction.

As a matter of fact, think of the timeshare example. Almost everyone that purchases a timeshare, purchases it within a 90-minute time span. Imagine that! People spend thousands of dollars on a product within a very short timeframe. Even cars are usually purchased in a longer timeframe. The main reason a lot of people purchase timeshares within such a short timeframe is because they have been emotionally engaged. The picture has been created, they have been placed in the picture, and the sales person has helped them to imagine themselves using the product. It is an emotional sale. I am not saying that there is anything wrong with purchasing in such a short timeframe. What I am saying is that most people like to take time to purchase products that cost a lot of money. So when exceptions are made it is usually because they have emotionally bought into it.

Employees can be engaged in the same way. Paint the picture with them. Allow them to imagine themselves in the picture. Make them feel as if they are an important part of the vision. Once employees have been stimulated, then they each need to be told what their role is in manifesting the vision. This is the opportunity to discuss values. This is the opportunity to discuss standards. This is the opportunity to discuss the equality and value of each individual and the company's commitment to partner with employees in helping them achieve their individual goals within the context of the organization. This is the ultimate opportunity to discuss the partnership and the mutual 'inclusivity' of both parties' goals. It is about communicating the philosophy that each individual is important, that their career needs are important, and also that the company wins when employees win. It means setting the foundation for the way forward and expressing the company's commitment toward new practices.

Communicating both the importance of the employees' role in achieving the company's goals, and the importance of helping employees achieve their own goals does two things: It makes employees feel as if they are an important part of something larger than themselves, while at the same time communicating a sense of support and concern for their individual needs and career goals. Communicating the company's goals, standards, and values, while at the same time expressing commitment to employees' development and achievement of their goals, creates an integral connection between employee and organizational goals.

Once employees are feeling a sense of value and inclusion, they are ready to lend their support to management. When employees are made to feel as if they are an integral part of an organization, buy-in is created and their level of motivation increases. However, at this point their support is conditional. It is based on the idea of WIIFM – "What's in it for me?" – not just in words, but also in practice. This is a prerequisite to getting employees' total buy-in. Therefore, just as communicating the vision is essential to getting employees' buy-in, practicing what has been espoused is just as essential to the buy-in process. So, if the vision of the organization has been shared in an inclusive manner, and the espoused values of the importance of employee goals are practiced, individuals are more likely to work toward achieving the organization's goals, especially if they know that achieving the company's goals means achieving their own goals.

Engage Employees

Following the discussion of the vision, employees should be engaged in creating the plan of action for reaching the company's goals within their departments. Individuals in each department should be encouraged to brainstorm on strategies for reaching their departmental goals. This can be valuable for several reasons: Employees are likely to identify strategies that executives may not think of because employees are involved in the daily operations; Employees are more likely to be committed to the implementation of the strategies because they have been involved in the process; And the strategies are their own ideas, which means an automatic buy-in to its success with the policing of each other to ensure compliance.

Chapter 6:   Operationalize The Strategy

"Setting a goal is not the main thing. It is deciding how you will go about achieving it and staying with that plan."

Tom Landry[7]

The next step is to put the strategies created by executives and employees into action. In many instances, the poor execution of business strategy is one of the major factors in strategy failure. Strategies have to be effectively translated into action. Now that you have departmental targets and strategies that will achieve the company's goals, it is necessary to create a departmental plan of action that will put the strategies into action.

Reminder: The goal of New Energy Enterprises (Wholesalers) is to reduce operational cost by 20% in 2009. Using their Accounts department as the example, if employees identified a strategy of increasing the collection rate of the Accounts Receivables section, a plan would be created for implementation. So, the plan might look like this (*see chart i*).

7   *Quote Source: http://thinkexist.com/quotation/setting_a_goal_is_ not_the_main_thing-it_is/151192.html*

In such a plan, all of the strategies should be listed as well as all of the steps required for strategy implementation. Additionally, job functions should be assigned to each step. A supplementary document may be required to provide a more detailed plan of steps and tasks that may be required for strategy implementation.

Chart I

NEW ENERGY ENTERPRISES (WHOLESALERS)

ACCOUNTS DEPARTMENT PLAN OF ACTION

COMPANY GOAL: Reduce operational cost in 2009 by 20%

ACCOUNTS TARGET: Reduce cost in 2009 by 10%

ACCOUNTS STRATEGIES:

1. Streamline accounting processes — Accounts Dept
2. Increase revenue collection rate by 30% — Accounts Receivables Section

PLAN OF ACTION:

Strategy 1 Accounts Dept.

Examples

- Determine efficiency targets by week 1. **(Supervisors)**
- Review all accounting processes to test efficiency levels by month 1. **(Supervisors)**
- Streamline processes to ensure alignment with efficiency targets by month 2. **(Accounting Officers)**

Strategy 2 Accounts Receivables Section

Examples

- Mail billing statements within 24 hours following customer charges. **(Receivables Assistants)**
- Place follow up collection calls within 10 business days of customer charges. **(Receivables Assistants)**
- Place additional follow up calls within 5 business days of initial collection call. **(Receivables Assistants)**

This sample plan is not complete. It is for illustration purposes only and may not represent true strategies or steps for goal achievement, nor ideal numbers or timeframes.

INDIVIDUAL WORK PLANS

An individual work plan needs to be developed for each employee. This will help to create a culture of accountability and focus individuals toward organizational objectives. These individual work plans would be blueprints for achieving the departmental targets and the company goals. They outline the employee's role and responsibilities for achieving business goals. It represents the employee's commitment to the company and fosters self-leadership. A sample is provided (*see chart ii*).

The Individual Work (IW) Plan should be in the form of measurable objectives. There should be objectives stated for each job function in the IW Plan. These objectives should align with the department's overall goal. The detailing of work objectives in measurable form is necessary for employees to become clear on their roles and the company's expectations of them. It is important that every job function expectation of employees be outlined in objective format with specific targets.

Chart II

NEW ENERGY ENTERPRISES (WHOLESALERS)

ACCOUNTS DEPARTMENT

RECEIVABLES ASST. INDIVIDUAL WORK PLAN

EMPLOYEE NAME

COMPANY GOAL: Reduce operational cost in 2009 by 20%

ACCOUNTS TARGET: Reduce company cost in 2009 by 10%

ACCOUNTS RECEIVABLES STRATEGIES:

1. Increase revenue collection rate by 30%

WORK OBJECTIVES FOR COLLECTION FUNCTION
(List not complete)

1. Develop task-timeline chart weekly.
2. Mail all billing statements w/in 24 hours following customer charges 96% of the time.
3. Place follow up collection calls to 98% of customers on your assigned list within 10 business days of the customer charge date.
4. Place additional follow up calls to 95% of customers within 5 business days of initial collection calls if payments were not received.

WORK OBJECTIVES FOR RECORD KEEPING FUNCTION

1. Update customer data section with each customer contact 100% of the time.
2. Etc.

_____   _____
   Employee Signature   Date

_____   _____
   Supervisor Signature   Date

This sample IW plan is not complete. It is for illustration purposes only and may not represent ideal numbers or true objectives for this work function.

In most cases, a perfect rate of 100% is not used in setting work plan objectives because employees are not perfect. If perfect rates are given, most employees will fall short of their targets and it can be considered a setup for failure, although, you do want them to deliver on the results 100% of the time. However, setting the mark at 95% encourages success and over achievement, while the use of 100% could be seen as a set-up for failure. If they perceive the targets to be impossible, such as '100% of the time,' they may not attempt to reach them because they perceive it as impossible to reach. It is better to set targets that can be reached and have rewards for over achievement. So it is wise to avoid setting 100% targets as much as possible.

Be flexible enough to align job tasks with employees' skills and interests as often as possible. For example, if you have two Accounts Receivables Assistants, and one enjoys making the collections calls while the other prefers the administrative tasks, separate the tasks accordingly and have it reflected on their Individual Work Plans. Be sure to have an open discussion with both individuals to look at the pros and cons of dividing the tasks in that way, and be sure to have their consent.

The Individual Work Plan is used as a tool to ensure that expectations are clear, and every step is outlined to ensure the achievement of the company's goals with an ultimate focus of creating self-leadership. This is the document that outlines how the employee will assist the company in reaching its strategic objectives and goals. Employees' acceptance of the objectives should be indicated by their signature on the IW Plan. The company's role in assisting employees to reach their goals will be discussed in a subsequent chapter.

However, creating a culture of self-leadership goes beyond creating individual work plans. It requires helping employees to learn the art of reviewing themselves in terms of their ability and work effectiveness. One responsibility that leaders have in promoting self-leadership is to show employees how to conduct analysis. One of the keys to an effective operation is having a strong ability to assess various organizational components and their impact on performance.

Employees must be trained on how to isolate performance challenges and to be in a constant mode of analysis. An analytical ability comes naturally to some, but it can be most challenging for others. So all of the necessary tools need to be provided to make it as easy as possible for employees to become self-leaders.

From an organizational perspective, a tracking report will need to be created for the Accounts department to keep a record of individual and departmental progress toward the goals. Such a report should reflect the overall goal, the departmental target, current collection rates, and monthly achievements both individual and departmental. There should also be a monthly review of progress and any necessary adjustments or tweaking of strategies to ensure achievement of the targets. These review sessions should involve employees in keeping with the philosophy of employee participation and partnership in reaching goals. These sessions will serve three purposes: 1. Help to keep track of the department's progress towards the overall goal; 2. Help to ensure that the strategies are effective; and 3. Help to keep employees motivated in achieving targets.

Individual targets should be carefully managed. Ensure that the targets are not overwhelming. Starting off moderately will help to ensure success. Individual targets should be reviewed on an ongoing basis and reset as necessary. A gradual increase in targets is sure to be far more effective in ensuring success than setting overly ambitious targets at the onset. Failure of employees to reach targets, if set too high too soon, could cause high levels of de-motivation and a sense of discouragement. Starting off with moderate target levels can help to keep employees motivated. Participants should always be set up to succeed and not to fail.

ITS APPLICATION

Essential to this approach of creating individual work plans, is the need to ensure that there are policy and procedures manuals for every department. This manual is essential for telling employees their partner's requirements, and it guides departmental strategizing and function to ensure the employer's expectations are met in the achievement of organizational objectives. It can be viewed as the employer's stipulation in the partnership agreement.

Some of the components of this model have been loosely structured to allow for individual company relevance. Examples were chosen to illustrate the point being made, even though some of the examples may not be relevant to your organization. Nevertheless, it is important to realize that every single job can be broken down into task objectives.

The sample goal of decreasing cost is not limited to the accounts department in its application. If this goal is relevant for your organization, objectives and strategies should be explored for each department. You would be amazed at some of the innovative ideas that can come out of a brainstorming session with employees. With this goal, all aspects of the organization should be reviewed with employees input to identify cost saving opportunities.

Whether each department's tasks tie directly into the company's overall strategic goal or not, each function needs to be set up with objectives in an Individual Work Plan. Effective organizational functioning is required in every area of the company to fulfill the company's purpose and achieve all organizational objectives and goals. Ultimately, all work functions tie into organizational success whether directly or indirectly.

Chapter 7: T 'N T — Tools & Training

"Our mission statement about treating people with respect and dignity is not just words but a creed we live by every day. You can't expect your employees to exceed the expectations of your customers if you don't exceed the employees' expectations of management."

Howard Schultz[8]

As previously stated, there are many things that impact an organization's performance. Therefore, organizational analysis and a review of the various systems are essential practices for the effectiveness of the new consciousness model. Every aspect of the organization must work together to ensure organizational effectiveness and achievement of the company's goals.

Employees must be given every opportunity to become self-leaders and to succeed with their work objectives by ensuring that they are given the tools and the support that is needed to perform their job functions effectively. This includes the right systems and processes, organizational structures, the necessary

---

8   *Quote Source: http://www.woopidoo.com/business_quotes/respect-quotes.htm*

47

procedures manuals, and a comfortable work environment. All of these various components are a part of the organizational system and can impact the organizational efforts positively or negatively.

If a departmental objective is to increase its efficiency, then a slow or outdated computer system does not allow the employees to perform at optimal levels and thus prevents them from effectively working toward their departmental targets. If the company's goal is to decrease the time from the point of sale to the delivery of goods, but the organizational structure does not allow for smooth transitions between departments, again it prevents employees from meeting the company's targets.

If one department is fully engaged in hitting its targets, its results can still be negatively impacted by the inadequacies of another department as is clearly demonstrated in the following example: The collections department of an organization was very focused on increasing their collection targets for a particular month. As most people know, it is very challenging to get customers to pay on delinquent accounts. Well, the employees got very creative in securing information and tracking down delinquent customers. However, when they contacted customers to come in and make payments some indicated that the lines were always too long, or that they can only come after 5pm, or they could only make a payment on a Saturday etc.

The staff members making these calls were very frustrated because they often complained to management that extended hours were needed in order to accommodate persons wanting to come in and make payments, but to no avail. They were discouraged in their efforts to hit departmental targets because no matter how well they did in reaching customers, the obstacle of the limited hours of the customer service department always had the potential to serve as an impediment to hitting their targets. And while it can be said that the customers may have only been using it as an excuse to avoid payments, I myself witnessed customers walking in the front doors and then walking right back out after observing the length of the customer service (cashiers) lines. The point is that at every juncture, employees must be given every opportunity to succeed.

And, executives should realize that not only is it essential to ensure that employees are always set up to succeed, but in business every effort must always be made to ensure that it is convenient for customers to make payments on invoices.

Training 101

Additionally, if individuals are expected to engage in new behaviors to improve organizational performance, one must ensure that they have the skills that will allow them to succeed. If training is required for any employees to effectively perform their function, then it is in the company's best interest to ensure that it happens. Using Accounts Receivables from the previous chapter as the example, individuals engaged in collections calls will need to understand the steps and strategies to perform this function. It is important for them to receive the basic training that may be necessary so that they are not set up to fail, but rather to succeed in reaching their targets.

Training is often considered a burdensome cost to companies that may or may not bring returns in the long run. This view is understandable given the many off-the-shelf training programs that are not effectively addressing employees' true training needs. However, it *is* possible to ensure that training is effective in helping the company achieve its goals, and this involves a number of steps. The following Training Effectiveness Steps apply generally, however each step may not always be applicable to each training need, and the relevance of each step is also dependent on each company's make-up and structure.

Training Effectiveness Step 1

Before determining that employees need training due to

performance challenges, make sure that you have ruled out any external factors that may be impacting performance. This of course does not apply to the need for skills training on new tasks. This point is generally more applicable to training needs that arise due to poor performance.

The first thing you have to do is determine whether the factors affecting performance are due to external conditions or internal conditions, or even a combination of both. Consider whether or not organizational performance is seasonal; consider if there have been changes in your marketing or advertising efforts; consider what's going on in the economy; and assess what new strategies the competition may be engaged in. The key is to first of all understand what external conditions may be impacting your business and thus departmental and individual performances.

Training Effectiveness Step 2

Before determining that an employee needs training due to performance challenges, make sure that you have ruled out any internal factors such as systems challenges, poor organizational structure, personality conflicts, etc. Otherwise, you could spend money on training and not address the real issues that are affecting performance. Here is an example of this point.

In an organization that I previously mentioned, in my division there was a department that was responsible for booking particular guest services each week. The Representatives' booking results fluctuated based on the number of hotel guests checking in each week and the results were analyzed weekly. During one period, executives were feeling optimistic because the busy season was starting. This meant that most weeks the hotel would be filled with guests and therefore booking results were expected to be outstanding. However, once the busy season started, the results revealed no real percentage change from the previous weeks in the services booked. Executives were upset and very concerned. Their immediate reaction was that the Representatives (reps) needed to be sent for training because the Executives felt that the reps should have had a major increase in the number of services they booked. In the minds of the Executives, how could the Representatives have possibly missed such a golden opportunity to increase their booking percentages?

I was also surprised and disappointed in the booking results because I felt the reps were fairly skilled in their jobs. What was even more puzzling was that they assured me that they booked almost everyone that they talked to. So, I decided to investigate further. Since the hotel was expected to be full the following weekend, I hung out in the hotel lobby to observe the Representatives in action.

What I discovered was interesting. It turns out that not all of the front desk clerks were sending the hotel guests over to the information desk to receive their free gift, which of course was a way to get the guests in front of the representatives, giving the representatives an opportunity to sell services. During slow times, the reps were able to stop the guests walking in and out of the lobby and offer guests their free gift, but during busy times the reps weren't always aware of all of the guests walking in and out of the lobby.

Based on my observations, I then created an incentive program to ensure that the front desk clerks remembered to send each guest over to the information desk for their free gift. It turns out that the Representatives were right. They were able to sell services to a high percentage of the guests that came to them, and their booking percentages increased dramatically after implementing the incentive program with the front desk clerks.

If the representatives were sent for training at the onset, it would have resulted in money spent on unneeded training, and continued poor performance. It is essential to always fully analyze performance challenges before deciding that training is needed.

Training Effectiveness Step 3

One has to assess the individual(s) first. Ensure that there actually is a skill deficiency and an actual need for training. There are several factors that impact an individual's work performance resident within the individual. These include the individual's level of motivation; their level of interest in the work; their knowledge base; their interpersonal communication and work style; and their skill set. The only time training is appropriate is when there is a need for new skills, although, training can address an individual's lack of knowledge. All of the other issues are related to the individual's goals or personal challenges, which will be addressed in the succeeding chapter.

Training Effectiveness Step 4

If you have determined that an individual or individuals lack the skills to perform their work functions, then you have to identify the specific challenges. This is vital and is often the point at which training mistakes are made. For example, you can have an employee whose function includes providing customers with basic information about a service that is provided; but every time that employee has to give information concerning quotes, they pass the caller on to someone else. The customer then gets frustrated because he or she can't seem to get the needed information in a timely manner. If this employee is generally a good employee and is fairly knowledgeable about your company's products, you may feel that she (*used for ease of reference*) simply needs training on how to deal with customers.

If you were to leave it at that and send the individual for

training, she may come back with an improved ability to handle customers: or, her customer service performance may be unchanged. Without having looked closer at the performance challenge, you could possibly have made a costly mistake. Looking more closely at the issue, you may discover that the specific challenge she has with giving quotes may be related to information not included in your list of prices, for example. It could be that she has no math calculation abilities. So, when the customer asks a question about a product package that involves possibly breaking out the individual components and combining other components, she simply does not know how to assist them.

This is a very different challenge than that of not knowing how to address or relate to customers. If the individual is sent for the wrong kind of training, not only can it be costly to the company, but she will still lack the right kind of training, and it can de-motivate and frustrate an otherwise good employee. Therefore, identifying the right training needs is essential.

Training Effectiveness Step 5

You must ensure that the training that has been identified is properly designed for the skill that is needed. A part of the challenge that many business executives face is that many training programs are not designed to meet their specific skill need. In many instances the training programs being utilized are off-the-shelf training programs that don't always address the specific issues of the organization using them. Once you begin with an inadequate training program, you are bound to continue on this path of ultimately not meeting the need for which your planned training was intended.

One way around this is to have a training program customized for your organization, which only makes financial sense if it is to address a wide scale organizational need; or have your trainer, who should be able to do this, tweak the off-the-shelf training program that is being used to ensure that the specific issues and needs of the individuals/organization are being addressed.

If none of these solutions are feasible, then make sure you review the training objectives of whatever training you are considering to assess what specific skill is being taught. (*Training objectives are expounded upon in the next step.*)

Training Effectiveness Step 6

You have to ensure that the training objective not only ensures learning, but that the expected results are measurable. And no matter what training occurs, you should *always* ensure that the objectives are designed to measure what they are supposed to measure, *and* that the objectives are measurable!

It is one thing to say for example, "by the end of this training, participants will have a more positive attitude towards work," and another thing to say, "By the end of this training participants will be able to demonstrate the proper way to greet customers based on the criteria set." The first objective is not measurable, the second is.

To make the first objective measurable, it would need to be, "by the end of this training, participants will be able to explain the importance of a positive attitude and demonstrate it in the workplace by being prompt, taking initiative, being accountable etc.," which may also require a set criteria defining the meaning of "accountability" and other measurables being used.

Also, remember to ensure that the objectives measure what they are supposed to measure. If the work and skill challenge is "not knowing how to fill a customer's work order," for example, then you have to ensure not only that the training is designed to teach this, but that a specific objective to measure the attainment of this is set also. Otherwise, you can have a great, measurable training objective, but it measures the wrong skill. In other words, ensure that your objective measures that for which the participants have received training, and not measure something for which they have not received training.

Training Effectiveness Step 7

You have to ensure that the learning process is actually a process that is proven to be effective in training individuals. For example, it is highly unlikely that if you stand in front of a group of training participants and lecture on the importance of a positive attitude that you will see any changes in behavior. This type of a performance challenge would require more in-depth discussions and participant interaction. It would require evoking emotions, and taking participants to some "ah ha" moments. To give another example, if you wanted to train individuals on the proper way to greet customers, you wouldn't just explain it to them. You would demonstrate it, and have them demonstrate it back to you and practice it.

Training Effectiveness Step 8

Ensure that the employee is motivated to incorporate or use her training at work. Increasing the probability that training participants will carry their new skills, knowledge, and behavior back to the workplace requires the use of some specific tools and strategies. First of all, the training objectives have to be set in a way that is easily transferable to the workplace.

Setting training objectives that are easily transferable to the workplace is a must in order to give the participants every opportunity to succeed. Let's use the example of a skill deficit that created the training need of 'not knowing how to complete a customer work order form.' If the training objective is, "by the end of this training participants will be able to demonstrate the correct way of completing a customer work order form," this objective would be both measurable and designed to measure what it is supposed to measure—completing a customer work order form. However, this training objective only covers the semantics on the work order form ensuring that participants know what information to put where on the form. This may not effectively address the training need.

In the workplace, the challenge may be that customers explain the problems that they are having to the customer service representative (CSR), but customers may then require the CSR to tell them what services they (customers) may need to address their problems. If the CSR does not know how to determine the service customers may need, this is a larger problem than 'not knowing how to complete a customer work order form.' In this case, understanding is required of both the problem and the appropriate service needed in order to correctly complete the customer work order form.

So, to fully address the training need, the training objective would need to change. A training objective that would be more complete and easily transferable to the workplace for the needed skill would be, "by the end of this training, participants will be able to: 1. Identify all of the problems that each of our services is designed to address as outlined on our service sheet; and 2. Appropriately and correctly complete a customer work order form.

The service sheet makes the skills easily transferable. If during the training there were just discussions about the types of problems customers face and the types of services offered to address them, this would not be enough. Do not force employees to memorize things that may not be necessary for them to memorize. Providing a service sheet that lists all of the possible problems and what services address each problem provides a reference and ensures that employees can succeed with their new skill. In time, they will come to know the information. So these new objectives not only ensure that the employees have received the right training, they provide an opportunity for employees to demonstrate their new ability following the training and an easy way to utilize their new skills/knowledge in the workplace.

Other points on ensuring that the employees are motivated to transfer their new skills to the work-place have already been addressed or will be discussed in subsequent sections. Nevertheless, they will be listed here for thoroughness:

- ◄ Participants should have a clear understanding of the vision of their organization and their role in getting there; Participants should be shown the connection between their new training and the overall vision of the company that was communicated to them earlier. This will help to maintain their level of motivation and continue to allow them to feel a part of the organizational efforts to achieve success.

- ◄ Participants should have a clear work plan that incorporates the training objectives; The Individual Work Plan that has been developed previously, should reflect the need for the use of the new skills. Otherwise, the IW Plan should be adjusted to include objectives based on the new training, which should tie into departmental targets and the company's overall goals.

- ◄ Participants' performance reviews should align with their individual work plans; Every Individual Work Plan should be aligned with the performance review and its process. The details of this will be outlined in the next chapter.

- ◄ And, once again, participants should be set up to succeed and not to fail with their new skills in the workplace. Once again, this relates to having the right tools to succeed and objectives (that are incorporated in the Individual Work Plan) not being set at 100% to measure success.

Various examples were used here to illustrate the training points and ensure clarity in discussions on training. However, some of these examples are not expected to arise when using this business model. This point will become clearer in subsequent discussions on the employee's perspective.

If these training guidelines are followed whenever a training need arises, the training will serve as an asset to the organizational functions and the achievement of the company's goals. If it is known at the onset that training will be required, ensure that the recovery of the training cost is included in the departmental targets set, so that it does not impact any gains made in cost reduction, for example.

Chapter 8: WIIFM—What's In It For Me?

"In business you get what you want by giving other people what they want."

Alice MacDougall[9]

It should be commonly understood that each of us makes decisions based on what's in our own best interest. This is the main motivator for our actions. Most individuals work because they need to make a living. Some individuals are lucky enough to work in professions that they enjoy and so they work for the love of it. Others find it an often unattractive necessity. These are the individuals that require major motivation to perform well. Although, there are some who perform well without external motivation because it is in their nature to do so, however, this is not so for most employees. Therefore, it becomes necessary to discover ways to motivate employees that are not cost prohibitive.

The mistake often made by many executives is to assume that money is the greatest motivator. However, there are a number of research studies that have proven otherwise, and

---

9   *Quote Source: http://www.myquotebox.com/Business-quotes.html*

suggest other types of things that truly motivate individuals. These things are also found to be effective within organizations and are mainly internal motivators like recognition, autonomy, work fulfillment etc. The bottom line is that the motivators for most individuals involve the same elements that relate to our humanness.

As humans, we like to be respected, appreciated, assisted, cared for, and given freedom to be who we are. These needs and desires do not go away when individuals become members of an organization. The belief that individuals can leave this outside the company's doors is absurd, yet it is commonly expected and attempted. This expectation is where many executives go wrong. You cannot ask individuals to stop being human. You cannot ask them to put aside who they are to become a robotic employee eight hours a day, five days a week, how ever many days a year, and then expect fantastic results. If this were easily achieved, there wouldn't be so many employee challenges in the workplace.

In my work as an Organization Development Consultant, every single client that brought me in to assess their employee-related organizational challenges shared a common thread—they had ignored the humanness factor. This was at the crux of each one of their challenges. Yes, the problems manifested themselves in different ways, but at the core were the employees' sense of feeling disrespected, unappreciated, and uncared for.

In these organizations, a major problem that occurred was miscommunication. Executives didn't really intend to disrespect employees and be unappreciative, but communications and actions can often be misinterpreted by employees, thus causing ill will. Employees choose how to interpret management's communications. If employees believe that management does not have their best interest at heart, they will interpret management's communications based on that premise. However, when management begins with the premise that employees are to be respected in the same manner that top executives are, they become more thoughtful of their communication and actions. And employees will perceive the communications accordingly. This is why this new consciousness model begins with the philosophical approach of viewing each employee as being just as important as the executive. This mind set is necessary because it helps to guide each communication and each action, and in this context, even subconscious communications occur in a mode of respect. Also, when employees generally believe that management has their best interests at heart, they often give them the benefit of the doubt even if communications are not totally positive.

CREATE A CULTURE OF PARTNERSHIP

And why not respect employees' needs and desires as much as your own or other top executives'? What does it take away from executives to do this? It costs nothing, but it does make your employees feel like partners in business with a sense of responsibility to do their part. A partnership approach can maximize organizational performance. The key to creating a culture of partnership began with the sharing of the company vision. It included having employees participate in the brainstorming of strategies. It also included creating a blueprint for them to succeed in achieving their departmental targets and the company's goals. However, this partnership is revealed best through the traditionally termed 'performance appraisal or review' process. This represents a grand opportunity to create a culture of partnership. Although, what is advocated in this model is a far cry from the traditional performance review process.

What's wrong with the traditional performance appraisal process?

Traditional review processes do not promote a culture of

partnership. It appears that too often supervisors or managers view the performance appraisal process as a time for punishment, criticism, or judgment. And while the process does involve evaluation of sorts, the focus should always be on the most effective way to achieve the objective—the objective being performance improvement or excellence in the workplace. If the objective is performance improvement, then every effort should be made to do just that—improve performance.

The problem with many of the performance review instruments being used in companies is the content itself, from two perspectives: 1. The relevance of the objectives or attributes listed on the instrument; and 2. The fact that the terms within the objectives or the attributes themselves are not defined. In my consulting practice, I have seen performance appraisal instruments or forms with objectives and attributes that are not at all relevant to the employee's specific job function. This is often because off-the-shelf performance appraisals are being used.

If you were to use a traditional performance appraisal instrument, although not advocated in this model, the objectives listed within a performance appraisal instrument should always be relevant and reflective of the employee's job function. Otherwise, the evaluation process defeats the purpose for which it was intended. Also, terms should be specifically defined. It is unfair and ineffective to evaluate individuals using generic terms whose meanings are left up to the individuals' imaginations.

For instance, many performance appraisal forms include a measure of 'positive attitude.' What exactly is 'a positive attitude?' Unless it is specifically defined and is measurable, the interpretation of 'a positive attitude' is subjective. If you wanted to evaluate 'a positive attitude' in a traditional sense, the term would need to be defined. For example: "demonstrates positive attitude by showing initiative, being punctual 90% of the time, etc."

In addition to the use of inappropriate instruments, the most counterproductive aspect of this process is the way many companies handle the process itself. Many employees view the performance appraisal process with dread and they sometimes act as if they are 'walking down the plank.' This is not because they feel they have performed badly. Rather, this dread is due to a sense of uncertainty because in many instances, employees don't know what to expect. This should never be the case. In some companies, the entire evaluation process has become perfunctory, which then begs the question, why bother? In a perfect world, I would structure the entire process differently in every company.

This new consciousness business model has no room for the traditional performance review systems. Instead of having the manager use the approach of being 'the big bad judge,' employees should rate themselves, but not in the way it is done now where employees are asked, "how do you think you did?" Instead, it is about a philosophy of employees setting work objectives that they feel they need to work toward, in conjunction with managers, and they (employees) themselves discussing their progress during the evaluation process. So instead of being 'the big bad judge,' the manager's approach is one of partnership: "I am here to support you, to coach you, and to help you achieve your goals." This approach fits within the wider philosophical approach inherent within the organization and is exactly what is advocated in this new consciousness model.

THE PARTNERSHIP

In a partnership, 'there is something in it for everybody.' In a partnership, everyone is accountable for bottom-line results. In a partnership, each partner is considered to be important. The attitude of being in a partnership during the review process is critical to this new consciousness business model.

In this approach, the performance review process has a different function. However, it serves the same purpose, which is to review performance and motivate employees to achieve organizational goals. Any type of performance review must be in alignment with this model's philosophy. It must reflect the attitude of partnership, therefore it must begin with a new label. Here are some options to be considered:

Partnership Review Session
Goals Review Session
Employee Development Session
WIIFM Session (What's In It For Me Session)

These are possible terms that can be adopted or any other that reflects the sense of equality of employees or the sense of 'support for employees' efforts.' If management has committed to this philosophical approach (and they must for its success) then it should be easy to naturally convey the attitude "I am here to support you and help you achieve your goals." Because, this is the WIIFM (*pronounced wiff-um*) Session. Remember the premise—'in order for me (Mr. Executive) to achieve my goals, you have to be able to achieve yours.' This is the session that communicates self-leadership and creates the foundation for employees to reach their goals. This session can be conducted by Human Resources or the department's supervisor; it doesn't matter because all executives are required to buy into the philosophy if employing this new consciousness business model.

STATEMENT OF RESPONSIBILITY

It is advocated that a "Statement of Responsibility" be created that each employee will have to sign upon employment with your company. This statement is a two-way street. It reflects the philosophy of partnership and is a commitment that each of the partners agrees to make with the other. The company agrees to honor the employee's goals, do all in its power to assist them, and remunerate them for their work performance; the employee agrees to be prompt, accountable, work the agreed upon hours, adhere to the company policies, and deliver on the work objectives created in partnership with the company. This document should have both the employee's signature and the company representative's signature. While this is an over-arching document outlining the general responsibility of each partner, there are two specific documents that arise out of this: The Individual Work Plan and the Individual Development Plan (*to be discussed*).

The above-mentioned are the two agreements that will help each of the partners to reach their individual goals. The Executive's document of agreement between the company and the employee is the Individual Work Plan developed in partnership with the employee. The employee's document of agreement between the employee and the company is their own goal achievement plan, the Individual Development Plan, developed with the human resources development practitioner upon arrival at the company (or at whichever point this model is being implemented).

The WIIFM Session has three essential components: Individual Development Plan review; Individual Work Plan Review; and Organizational Resolutions.

INDIVIDUAL DEVELOPMENT PLAN REVIEW

An Individual Development (ID) Plan must be developed in the first WIIFM session held with each employee. This session should discuss the company's philosophical approach, which should be one of partnership, and then discuss the employee's goals for him/herself. It is important to note that the HR practitioner or Supervisor facilitating this session should not be judgmental about any objective or goal put forward by the employee.

It is the employee's choice. If an employee has absolutely no ambition and is simply there to obtain a paycheck, that should also be acceptable. As long as she (*for ease of reference*) fulfills her agreement with the IW Plan it should be acceptable. There is still an opportunity to help motivate her to perform well. Remember, it is about being human—being treated with respect and being appreciated, no matter their choices. However, know that all individuals will not be a good fit with this approach and so one should not hesitate to end the partnership if it becomes necessary. Nevertheless, even individuals with no ambition would prefer to enjoy what they do, as opposed to not enjoying it, and can still participate in a valuable manner.

The ID Plan should have the employee's goals, objectives/steps for getting there, as well as a development plan. (*See chart iii and chart iv for two sample plans.*)

Chart III

SAMPLE*

NEW ENERGY ENTERPRISES (WHOLESALERS)

JANE SMITH

INDIVIDUAL DEVELOPMENT PLAN

EMPLOYEE GOAL: Gain 5 years experience in General Accounting

OBJECTIVES

1. Gain 2 years experience in Accounts Receivables
2. Gain 2 years experience in Accounts Payables
3. Gain 1 year experience in Payroll

DEVELOPMENT STRATEGIES:

EDUCATION DESIRED: Complete Bachelor Degree by 2012

TRAINING REQUIRED: 1. Accounts Payables internal training
                        2. Payroll Training

EMPLOYEE COMPENSATION

CURRENT JOB FUNCTION: RECEIVABLES ASSISTANT

CURRENT SALARY: $29,000 Annually

BENEFITS: Insurance Coverage, 2 weeks vacation, 3 days study leave annual

SALARY GOAL: $32,000 BY 2010

SALARY GOAL STRATEGY

➢ Surpass work objectives' targets
➢ Be personally responsible for 3% reduction in cost of departmental targets.
➢ Complete required training before job reclassification at 2009 year end.

_____   _____
Employee Signature   **Date**

_____   _____
Supervisor Signature   **Date**

**This sample ID plan is for illustration purposes only and may not represent ideal or true salaries
or goals for this job function.*

Chart IV

SAMPLE*

NEW ENERGY ENTERPRISES (WHOLESALERS)

SALLY JOHNSON

INDIVIDUAL DEVELOPMENT PLAN

EMPLOYEE GOAL: Increase salary annually

OBJECTIVES

1. Receive maximum increases annually
2. Achieve bonuses whenever available

DEVELOPMENT STRATEGIES:

EDUCATION DESIRED: None

TRAINING REQUIRED: Accounts Receivables Basics

EMPLOYEE COMPENSATION

CURRENT JOB FUNCTION: RECEIVABLES ASSISTANT

CURRENT SALARY: $27,000 Annually

BENEFITS: Insurance Coverage, 2 weeks vacation

SALARY GOAL: Maximum Annual Increases

SALARY GOAL STRATEGY

➤ Achieve work objectives targets
➤ Complete required training before year end

_____   _____
    Employee Signature   **Date**

_____   _____
    Supervisor Signature   **Date**

This sample ID plan is for illustration purposes only and may not represent ideal or true salaries or goals for this job function.

Both of the sample plans reflect the same subsections, however the employees' choices are different. Jane Smith has set targets for herself of completing five years experience and obtaining a Bachelor's degree. Sally Johnson simply wants to obtain as high a salary as possible. (In the sample, the difference in starting salaries is a reflection of the education levels of the two employees upon entrance to the company, and the difference in benefits for Jane Smith is based on her negotiation for study time when the job was offered.)

Despite the difference in employee goals and ambition levels, there is no reason why both individuals cannot work optimally to achieve Individual Work Plan objectives and departmental targets. Although the temptation may be to do otherwise, both employees should be treated with the same respect and given the same opportunities to perform optimally because in this context, they will both help the company to reach its goal. Nevertheless, inherent in the employee ID Plan is the opportunity for the company to give back for exceptional work. i.e. Jane Smith desires the opportunity to work in other job functions while employed at the company as a part of her individual goal. In order to achieve this, the company will have to allow or create the opportunity for her to move into the other areas. Remember, this is a partnership, and facilitating work experience in other areas for Jane is the company's part of the agreement.

Also, there may come times when it is discovered that an employee is a square peg being forced into a round hole. Because of your commitment to the philosophy that employees' goals are just as important as the company's, this challenge has to be addressed. If there is an opportunity for the individual to move into another area more suited for that individual's skill set and interest, then by all means facilitate it. If it can easily be created and fitted within the budget, then create the opportunity. If there is absolutely no opportunity for that skill set, allow the individual to make the decision to remain with the company or not. However, communicate that if he or she stays, he or she must be able to fill his or her end of the agreement in terms of their IW Plan.

A word of warning: Do not assume that an individual who performs poorly in one area is a poor performer in every other area too! A case in point: While I was working for a previously referenced company, there were two individuals that were fired from one of the departments for poor performance. Both of these individuals approached me and asked if they could volunteer in my division. I was a bit wary at first because I assumed, like many executives would, that they were not competent workers. Nevertheless, I listened to their reasons for wanting to do this and agreed to allow them to volunteer in my office for a short period of time.

I gave these individuals several tasks to perform and they came back several days later with these tasks completed. Not only did they complete two of the tasks based on my specific requirements, but they also created a new system that would make it easier to perform the tasks in the future and easier to give an analysis of the important components. I was totally blown away by this. I determined who was responsible for what aspects, and after determining where I could find space in my budget, I created two new positions within my division based on their skill set. They become two of my top performing employees from that point forward. In fact, one of them rose to become my right hand person. This was a very valuable lesson for me that I hope can benefit other executives as well.

A final note: Individual Development Plans should be reviewed and updated on an ongoing basis in terms of the employee's goals and objectives. The frequency of reviews and resetting of Individual Work Plan objectives should be based on the appropriateness and particular needs of the company.

INDIVIDUAL WORK PLAN REVIEW

Following the review of the Individual Development Plan during the WIIFM session, the Individual Work Plan should be reviewed and discussed. This aspect of the session should be conducted in conjunction with or by the department's supervisor, as he or she will be more familiar with the work function and targets. The purpose of the session is two-fold: 1. To assist the employee in reviewing his or her performance; and 2. To acknowledge, recognize and praise the employee's efforts. Given these objectives, the tone of this session is especially important. Once again, the role of the supervisor is the same—"How can I support you in your efforts?" A copy of the tracking report should be reviewed so that the employee can review her achievements.

In this session, the HR Practitioner/Supervisor is a facilitator in the true sense of the word. She is to provide support and input when asked, but is not to pass judgment on the employee's performance. When a role of support is used with an individual, that individual feels comfortable and free to assess himself/herself. This approach will yield far better results than if a supervisor was to stand in judgment of the employee's performance.

While true facilitation can be maximized with some training, remembering the philosophy of partnership and a 'your goals are important' approach will help a supervisor to easily serve as a facilitator. Nevertheless, an important tool that can be used in such a session is to do a lot of parroting and/or paraphrasing. i.e. repeating and summarizing what the employee has said. This encourages individuals to continue expressing themselves. Also, if the conversation seems stuck, get it going again by asking non-threatening questions focused on the employee's achievements. i.e. "What was it like to hit your target in September?" If she feels comfortable with you and you are focusing on her triumphs, no matter how minute, she will eventually move to the areas where or the months when her performance may have fallen short. Once she has brought up her poor performance level, then you can ask questions like, "What do you think was different this month?" and "What do you think you would like to do differently?"

The latter question is only non-threatening if it is asked in this context at this point of the discussion. If you start off the discussion with this question, it is accusatory and will immediately cause the individual to clam up because she feels attacked. It also helps that you have discussed her goals during the first part of the session, which suggests that her needs are important. It communicates, "We care about you." The key to a successful session is the ability to be a good listener, for this is what allows individuals to develop a comfort level, which allows them to be prepared to assess themselves and work through their challenges.

What the individual should receive from the review of her IW Plan is a sense of appreciation, recognition, and motivation to improve her performance. She should also receive tips, suggestions and additional tools that can assist her in hitting her targets. If the individual has achieved any of the rewards (*see Chapter 9. Organizational Milestones*) as a result of outstanding performance with her individual objectives, this is also the time to congratulate her and reset objectives with higher targets, if she desires.

HOW CAN I MAKE YOUR JOB EASIER?

The final part of the session should focus on what you as the facilitator can do from an organizational perspective to make the job easier. This is to allow for any personality challenges, work environmental challenges, or even personal challenges to be resolved. Remember, the organization is a system of interrelated parts, and any part can negatively or positively affect performance. This approach and discussion allows the individual to truly see you as a partner in helping her to reach her goal and can work quite effectively.

Some years ago when I had received my first managerial post, I was quite worried about how I would get the employees in my division to work with me. I was new to the organization and young in age. Most of the supervisors in my division were older in years and had been with the organization for a very long time, and now I was to become their manager. There was talk among them that I was too inexperienced for the promotion. I knew I had to find a way to get these supervisors to respect and cooperate with me. This was crucial because my first assignment as a manager was a major task that required their input and support to get it done. So, I decided to go in with an attitude of 'I am here to serve you.' In my first meeting with each of the supervisors, I said, "How can I make your job easier?" And I kept that attitude in all of my dealings with them. Not only did they cooperate, but they also went around extolling my virtues to everyone.

At the time, I felt it was a risky approach because I thought 'I am their boss,' but I discovered that being their boss doesn't have to mean using a stick to get things done. Once again, employees are human. They want to be treated with respect, and they want you to care about their needs. They want to feel that they are just as important as you are within an organization.

This approach allows employees to become comfortable with their supervisor and focus more on achieving the organizational objectives because employees don't have to spend time 'keeping their walls up' because of feeling threatened. With this approach, they don't have to exist in fear or work from a perspective of 'it's me against the establishment.'

At times, there will be a need to remind employees of the commitment they made in their Statement of Responsibility. However, the 'how' is most important. One of the key things to making this model work is to not be so focused on the small things that it negatively impacts performance results. For example, obsessing with someone occasionally coming to work late. If an employee is over performing on their IW Plan, and the lack of promptness is not causing any undue hardship, then this is incidental. While their agreement to be accountable as outlined in the Statement of Responsibility is essential, do not allow such a matter to derail the employee's efforts and results. Such matters in general should be handled with this philosophical approach always in mind.

This is the perfect time to ask the question, "How can I make your job easier?" This approach invites the individual to open up about the lateness to work. You may find that what happened during those times were legitimate incidences that could not be avoided. Or, you may have an opportunity to help the individual strategize to avoid such occurrences in the future. The key is to discuss it in a way that is non-threatening and to ensure that you are seen as a partner wanting to assist in truly making things easier, especially if the individual's lateness has no negative impact on work performance. However, I recognize that there will be times that it can have a negative impact on work performance. Then strategies need to be discussed to address it. Nevertheless, the same attitude of 'how can I make your job easier' should be employed when discussing this. More serious challenges that require drastic action will be discussed in a subsequent chapter.

The WIIFM session with the Individual Development Plan is the employee-related aspect of this new consciousness model. The partnership agreement represented by the Individual Work Plan and Individual Development Plan must have equal focus in terms of level of importance, as both are essential components of this model. The sense of leadership and self-leadership makes this partnership complete. Diagram 2 reflects the relationship of the various components in this new consciousness model.

Diagram 2

A Different Path
New Consciousness Model

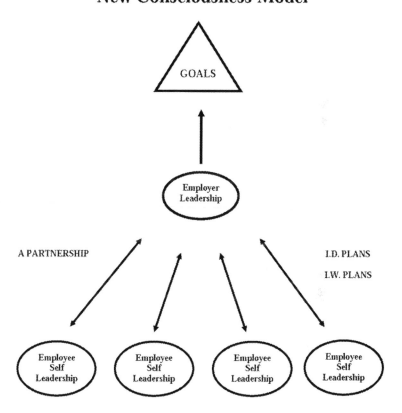

THE GOALS OF BOTH PARTNERS CAN BE MUTUALLY INCLUSIVE

Chapter 9: We Did It!

"There are two things people want more than sex and money -- recognition and praise."

> Mary Kay Ash, Founder, Mary Kay Cosmetics Inc.[10]

"The deepest principle in human nature is the craving to be appreciated"

> William James[11]

ORGANIZATIONAL MILESTONES

Celebration milestones are imperative for the effective use of this approach. Acknowledging accomplishments and celebrating achievements make us feel valued as individuals and help keep us motivated to have more achievements. An organizational milestone plan should be developed that includes an organizational milestone chart outlining targets with dates and a progress bar. The plan should include quarterly goal

---

10   *Quote Source: http://humanresources.about.com/od/leadership/a/ leader_reward.htm*

11   *Quote Source: http://www.brainyquote.com/quotes/quotes/w/ williamjam125466.html*

review dates, rewards and celebration plans. While this aspect can occur at an organization-wide level, monthly reviews should occur within each department.

Keep in mind that the milestone that is set and achieved will be different for each department and based on each department's function. And while all of the departments are not always going to be involved directly in every organizational strategy, each department's effective functioning contributes to your bottom line and therefore they all can participate in organization-wide strategy. All it requires is individual tailoring in terms of measurement for each department.

For example, while a receptionist can participant in cost cutting measures directly, she may not directly tie into the sales achieved by the sales department. However, this does not mean that she should not participate in an organization-wide strategy to increase sales. She can also tie into sales targets.

It requires first of all determining all of the contributing factors to a sale. If a potential client walks in the front door and is ill treated by the receptionist, he is likely to think twice about purchasing any product or services from that company; His thought might be "maybe this is the way the company feels about its clients." Therefore, targets like, smiles at clients 98% of the times; greets client pleasantly 98% of the times; offers clients refreshment 98% of the times etc. might be the measures used for a receptionist. It is important to involve every department in some form in organizational strategy because, and it cannot be stated too often, everything affects everything else within an organization.

Department heads should have monthly reviews of department's targets. As partners in this endeavor, these sessions should be done with employees as a group. It should not be a 'judgment' session, but rather an analysis of the progress being made. Individuals can be recognized for outstanding achievements, but all effort should be made not to put any one employee 'on the spot.' In fact, all employees should be made to feel as if their efforts are appreciated, regardless of their performance thus far. (Poor performance will be addressed subsequently.) This will serve to encourage better performance as opposed to causing discouragement and the desire to give up.

The department's monthly session is also an opportunity to review the strategies and replace the ones that are not effective, as well as adjusting targets if necessary. If any particular tool is working more effectively than others, this is an opportunity to share this information. It can also serve as a practice session or training session, such as on collection techniques using the Accounts Receivables example. After all of the various reviews, try to end the session on an upbeat, rallying note to have employees leave the session feeling renewed motivation to work toward their targets.

One thing that could entice employees and have them look forward to these sessions is to have refreshments and desserts to serve following the session. Food always connotes a party atmosphere at work. However, be sure to not have the cost of this become a burden on the company and its targets. In fact, you can have employees donate a couple of dollars a week to a refreshment fund and use that for monthly celebrations. You could also ask for a volunteer to bake a cake each month. People are more willing to participate and give in a partnership.

The Organizational Milestone Plan should have quarterly targets for the company goals with specific steps for assessing the progress. This progress should be communicated to the employees on a quarterly basis and should include recognition and reward components and celebration events. While it should not be cost prohibitive, these celebration milestones are essential to continued motivation and a sense of accomplishment. This will encourage employees to continue to work hard toward the company's goals. Costs for the Organizational Milestone Plan (The Plan) should be budgeted, as it is essential to this approach and business model.

The Plan could even include a bonus structure. I often

suggest to companies that there should be minimum targets that employees are required to meet and then additional targets that include a bonus structure (which should be taken from amounts exceeding bottom-line requirements) for excelling beyond the base targets. This of course encourages employees to exceed management's expectations.

Alternatively, a scoring system could be used. Points could be assigned to various target levels, and these points given to departments based on the target levels achieved. These points can be used for employees to receive an additional day off or vacation day for example. The reason this can work well is because employees working with Individual Work Plans are accountable for their performance themselves. Having an extra day off does not necessarily interfere with their targets. They still have to hit their targets within a given month and will work toward that despite their absence on a given day.

While this may be easy for an accounts department, for example, it may work differently for departments that have different structures. For instance, a customer service representative may have targets such as a 20% increase of 'add on sales' or an average rating of 8 (out of 10) on customer satisfaction surveys, etc. These representatives will still be able to work towards their monthly targets even with extra time off, but the scheduling of the time would have to be carefully thought out so services and the availability of customer services representatives are not negatively impacted.

These points could also be used for individuals that have goals of moving into different areas of work. Achievement of a certain amount of points could be required for having an opportunity to work within a different area. Although this should not be the only way someone is allowed to move to a different area, it could be considered a fast track method. For example, Jane Smith could use her points, if achieved, to start gaining the accounts payables experience she desires as outlined in her Individual Development Plan.

These points could also be used to represent employees excelling far beyond the targets and assisting with job reclassification decisions, promotion decisions, or salary increase decisions. However, all of these uses must be spelled out and communicated to employees prior to implementation. The bottom line is to think outside of the box on reward ideas that are not cost prohibitive and can help to serve the company further. A plan must be created that outlines a complete organizational milestones program.

Chapter 10: The Invisible Elephant

"The most important thing in communication is hearing what isn't said."

Peter F. Drucker[12]

Changing The Corporate Culture

Now that some of the formal structures have been addressed, it is necessary to look at organizational influences that are not so concrete, such as your organizational culture. An organization's culture represents the general thinking, or consciousness, of its members. It conceptually holds the accepted belief systems about the organization's practices, values and expectations. While an organization's culture is not a tangible thing, its power for 'good or evil' is real. The belief systems embedded in an organization's culture are far more influential than any written down rules of the organization, as the following story indicates.

I was consulting at a particular organization, and was talking to one of the mid-level managers, named Matt, about the fact

12   *Quote Source: http://humanresources.about.com/od/ interpersonalcommunicatiol/a/quotes_nonverb.htm*

that all managers appear to never leave the office before 7pm. I wanted to know if this was contractual. He explained that it was not in fact contractual, but something that all managers did because it was expected of them. The actual work hours were 8:30 to 5pm. Then he described his induction into that culture club.

Matt explained that on his first day at the company, he noticed that at five o'clock none of the other managers seem to be leaving the office. So, he decided to stay awhile. He worked until about 6pm and was feeling pretty good about establishing the fact that he was not a clock-watcher. The very next day he did the same thing. On the third day, as he was packing up to leave at 6pm, one of the managers came to him and told him that managers were expected to work at least until 7pm. Matt asked the manager why. The manager's response was that leaving before 7pm was frowned upon by the company's top executives.

Well, naturally Matt conformed, like most new employees do when they are told, "that's not the way we do things around here." Matt worked until 7pm daily like all of the other managers, however he indicated that he refused to work any later. Some of his colleagues worked even later than seven, all in an attempt to out-do each other. The perception was that the managers working the latest were the ones that would 'find favor with the gods,' thus landing on the fast track for promotion.

This perception, these expectations, and their practices were not written down rules within the organization, yet they controlled the behavior of its members. Company executives created a culture of conformity with the mistaken expectation that it would increase productivity. The challenge, however, with such a creation is that it doesn't necessarily get you the desired result. While you may think it is a good thing that all of your managers are working late, what exactly are they doing between the hours of 5pm and 7pm? Are they working, or are they finding non-productive things to occupy their time for appearances sake? If I were forced to work late for no sound reason, I would fake it.

The company might have been better served by encouraging their managers to leave the office on time. It would be better to allow managers time to de-stress and enjoy their time off so that they could return refreshed and ready to offer quality service as opposed to quantity of service. Company executives were successful in creating a culture of long hours, but to what end?

Some executives consciously create their organizational culture; for others, an organization's culture is like the invisible elephant in the room that you can't see but know is real, and because it is intangible, you have no idea what to do with it. Nevertheless, it cannot be ignored or artificially manipulated because it can have dire consequences for your organization, as in the following example.

One of my former clients had come up with a new strategy to try and get employees without first level degrees to continue their education. So they established an education reimbursement program and created a new promotion policy — all promotions would require a first level degree. Sounds good so far right? Well a number of problems arose from this:

1. Some entry-level staff members indicated that they were not making enough money to actually be able to afford paying school fees up front.
2. Other staff members that could afford it were not motivated to pursue it because...
3. The organizational policy of requiring a degree for promotion was not adhered to in the promotion of several individuals, and...
4. A number of individuals with degrees pursuing promotional opportunities were continuously denied promotions.

Remember, employees watch management's actions closely and this is what forms the opinions held by employees. The moment management dismissed the new policy to make exceptions for certain individuals the policy lost its effectiveness. However, the main culprit in the failure of the strategy was the lack of consideration of the existing organizational culture. The employees believed that anything requiring management approval would be given or approved if that employee 'found favor with the gods.' In other words, no matter what the policy, the perception was that managers were not objective creatures.

They knew 'favorability' was the real determinant of a promotion, so they ignored anything that said otherwise. What entrenched this belief into the culture of 'how things are done' were the actual practices of management. In a number of incidences, persons without degrees were promoted, and individuals with degrees were actually passed over for promotion. These occurrences, whether legitimate or not, reinforced the beliefs in the culture of 'the way we do things' much more than belief in any written down rules.

Once again, everything within an organization affects everything. If you know that you have a culture where employees question the objectivity of some mangers based on past practices, you can't expect new rules to wipe the slate clean, especially if the old practices of management are not cleaned up. When attempting to implement a new strategy or bring about change, you cannot ignore the existing work culture and the aspects that could influence your strategy.

Make The Elephant Your Friend

Changing an organization's culture can be one of the most challenging endeavors of an executive. Nevertheless, however challenging, it is not impossible. The first step is to discover what your culture says about your organization.

The culture of an organization tells the true story of the organization. If you want to discover the real company, pay attention to the things that are told to new employees. While not always the creators of the work culture, the employees are its administrators and they train their fellow workers. The socialization into the organization's culture usually starts with "that's not the way we do things around here," or "this is the way we do things around here." Cultural practices can range from courtesies as simple as, "the last person in the office usually turns off the coffee pot," to expectations as complex as "if our department has a major deadline, whether you are responsible for any of the project tasks or not, you are expected to work late to help complete the project."

As you know, organizational cultures have positive influences as well as negative influences on its members. The key is to minimize the negative influences and maximize its positives. One thing you don't ever want to do is to try and artificially manipulate your organization's culture with pretend practices. In other words, if company executives view employees as a means to an end, but they attempt to portray a concern for employees by implementing an employee program, that program will not necessarily translate to 'value of employees.' New policies and programs in and of themselves cannot change employees' perceptions and the resulting organizational culture.

Whatever is done for employees has to be real. If you are pretending, you are sure to be found out because no one can pretend 100% of the time. If you can truly adopt this philosophy of viewing every individual employee's goal as just as important as your company's, then changing the corporate culture can happen easily and is likely to happen naturally.

Because culture is not based on written down rules, employees' perceptions become very important in shaping culture. If the message being continuously communicated is that "we value employees and see them as equal; we respect employees in their ability to be self-leaders," this is what will shape your culture. When you share your company's vision with employees, and show them how they can help you achieve it, this communicates a partnership. When you develop individual work plans to show employees their role in achieving company objectives, this communicates responsibility. When you ask employees for their opinions on strategies and direction, this communicates trust. When you ask employees what their personal work goals are, this communicates concern for their lives and their future. When you celebrate employee achievements, this communicates appreciation and gratefulness. When these messages are continuously being communicated in your every organizational action, a conducive and positive work culture will result. It will evolve into a positive work culture because of what employees will perceive to be the truth about executives, management and the company as a whole.

Beware Of Conflicting Cultural Themes

A word of caution: All of your efforts can go to waste if you have conflicting themes influencing your organizational culture. If you have created a culture where the focus is on partnership, self-leadership, responsibility, appreciation etc., an opposing theme of competition, for example, can derail your best efforts. Competition is not congruent with "we are all equally important in our goals," and "we are each just as valuable as the next in our contribution." While many may view competition as producing great results, the context within which it is used is very important. Remember my client where the employees of a particular department were so focused on being seen as the 'favored' that they kept all of their clients to themselves, despite the client's interest in the services of other departments? In this example, the competitive practices resulted in missed opportunities for revenue creation because employees refused to share their clients with other departments.

If you are trying to create a culture of cooperation and partnership, which this model's philosophy extols, then the element of competition is not conducive to your organization. You may feel that competition drives productivity, but in this context, it will work to undermine your efforts for a new approach to business. While you can celebrate outstanding achievements, it is important to celebrate each individual's achievement at the same time. If, as an employee, I am never capable of performing at the same level as a co-worker, and you make that co-worker the standard for all others, I will give up my efforts. Most humans don't attempt the 'seeming' impossible because they do not like to fail. And everyone will never perform at the same level at similar tasks.

Another consideration for leaders is to be aware of the way external stakeholders are treated. If you are attempting to communicate a concern for others and wanting this to be representative of your work culture, but you treat suppliers poorly, or could care less about the customer's experience, it negates the message 'we care about you.' Once again, employees will believe what they see and not what they hear. As expressed by Ralph Waldo Emerson, "What you do speaks so loudly that I cannot hear what you are saying."[13] And while you are thinking that your internal efforts are creating the right organizational culture, poor treatment of the external stakeholders can create negative perceptions and be the determinant of cultural themes. Employees will not believe that you care about them if you don't care about the others. They will choose to believe that you care about no one.

Having said all of this, know that you may not always be aware of cultural themes. It is not always possible to know what is in the minds of employees from pure observation. You may think you are doing a fantastic job as a leader, only to later discover that your employees feel differently. Our best

13   Quote Source: http://humanresources.about.com/od/ interpersonalcommunicatiol/a/quotes_nonverb.htm

efforts can sometimes be misinterpreted. So, make the invisible elephant your friend. Make it a point to conduct on-going surveys, but not so often that employees get tired of them. Ask employees themselves what they perceive the company's values, focus, and unwritten rules to be. You will be amazed at how telling this can be.

I once had a client that asked me to come in and conduct a post-merger assessment of their organization. They had morale issues, but they didn't quite understand why. As always, the first thing I did was to conduct an assessment. I usually start with getting the executive/s' opinion on the organizational direction and their view of employees; then I move on to get the employees' opinion on the organizational direction and their view of executives. The most shocking discovery to the executives in this case was the fact that their employees, including middle management, had different views from executives about what the organizational direction was and what its main objectives and values were. How can an organization move ahead if its employees feel that the organization is heading in one direction, and its leaders feel it is heading in another? The interesting thing to executives was the fact that the staff members of the two merged companies were in agreement, and the executives of the two merged companies were in agreement, so the difference was at the employee level and not with the individual merged companies.

Executives were amazed by these discoveries because they thought they had done a great job of communicating with staff about the merger and their new goals two years prior, and they thought that they had a fairly good read on their staff members. However, the employees were forming opinions based on their perceptions. They watched the changes that took place to tell them where they were headed. They had opinions about the practices and procedures that were being slashed and the new ones that were being introduced, and these were the things that told them the direction of the company and not what executives wanted them to believe. Executives forgot how much perceptions determine reality for staff. And they failed to take into account issues such as human nature during a change process, the power of buried emotions about unresolved issues, and the barriers that can be created when employees feel insecure and unsafe about their jobs.

My point is that, once again, even the best intentions can go awry. It is always smart to have a reading of your organizational culture. The best way to handle the elephant in the room is to know as much about it as you can. This way, you can allow it to perform tricks and entertain you as opposed to stampeding and destroying your room—your organization.

Chapter 11: No Sticks, Just Carrots!

"...perhaps the most distinguishing trait of visionary leaders is that they believe in a goal that benefits not only themselves, but others as well. It is such vision that attracts the psychic energy of other people, and makes them willing to work beyond the call of duty for the organization."

Mihaly Csikszentmihalyi[14]

A lot has been said throughout this book about the need for leaders in organizations as opposed to managers. What exactly is a leader? There are countless discussions on the traits of leadership and whether leaders are born or made. However, I shall not engage in this discussion. What I will tell you is that I have had an experience that convinced me that I was working with a true leader. Here is my story.

A few years back, I attended a cocktail reception hosted by a new political party. The friend who had invited me was attempting to recruit me for the organization. I had absolutely no intentions of joining a political organization. My sole intent was to get out of the house to socialize a bit. Well, once I got there and heard the leader speak, something very different

---

14   *Quote Source: Good Business: Leadership, Flow, and the Making of Meaning,Page 197 http://www.gaia.com/quotes/topics/organization*

happened. It wasn't so much the man himself, but what he was saying. For the first time in my adult life, I heard a politician present really progressive ideas for the future.

My past experience had been hearing politicians espouse the same old rhetoric, which always sounded like an empty barrel of noise to me. However, this individual talked about implementing policies and instituting programs that made sense and addressed a number of challenges being experienced by the city. His ideas were innovative yet practical, and while he may not have been totally an 'Obama' in speech making, he spoke with a passion that I had seldom seen and with a sincerity that was obvious.

Well, needless to say I was moved. And while I am no idealist, I felt compelled to join their efforts to 'make the world a better place.' I almost felt obligated because of a famous quote that I had heard from one of my graduate school professors some years back. I don't remember the author, but the quote was, "if you are not a part of the solution, you are a part of the problem." That has always stuck with me and I use it in my approach to my life. So here I was confronted with the truth about me. If I was not a part of this solution before me, I would be a part of the problem. You see, I believed that the solutions presented were the best ones for moving the country forward. So if I didn't become a part of that drive, in my mind I would lose the right to ever complain about the supposed leaders and politicians of the country. Therefore, I joined the organization.

Shortly after that night, I had an experience that confirmed my decision as being the right one. A few members from the organization traveled to another city to have a small town meeting. An hour before the meeting the leader called us into his hotel room to say a few words. He said that no matter how many people showed up to the town meeting, we would do what we came to do. His exact words were, "If one person shows up tonight, we will give them the same message, the same enthusiasm, the same appreciation and energy, that we would give if one hundred people show up or if two hundred show up." I was literally stunned by this. In a hotel room with eight of his organizational members, this leader expressed the need to be true to our cause no matter what the number in the audience.

I had never heard of such commitment and determination to deliver on a presentation in the face of the potential challenge of one audience member even with no press expected at the event. That night, I realized his sincerity, his commitment, and his desire to bring about positive change. Throughout my time with this organization, I continued to be impressed with his leadership.

As I worked on this book, I knew I didn't want to engage in the usual discussion on what leadership is and is not, yet the idea of leadership could not be left out of this discussion. So I thought I would present an example of leadership that encapsules the philosophy of this approach. There were a number of things that this experience showed me about effective leadership.

People often commented on this new political party and the sentiment was that third parties never succeed; third parties are spoilers; this third party was a party of intellectuals that could never gather enough grassroot support, etc. They also questioned why the loyalty of its members were so strong. After our devastating losses in the general elections, people expressed surprise at the continued commitment and loyalty of the members to the leader. But there were a number of things they did not know about this leader.

This leader was able to win the loyalty of his members for several reasons:

1. He led the organization with a strong belief in the objectives of the organization. He truly believed that our goals were absolutly necessary and in the best interest of the people. This allowed him to be sincere and to communicate his sincerity in every speech. And because he believed so strongly in our cause, we the

members believed strongly in our cause and in him to help us achieve our goals.

2. He expressed true passion for the ideals and goals of the party to improve the lives of others. No one doubted his concern for people and the challenges faced by so many because he often demonstrated this. No matter what the outcome, he was always committed to addressing issues of concern to the public. And his passion was contagious.

3. He created a partnership. He involved his members in every aspect of the organization. He always made it about us. He never made <u>any</u> decision without listening to input from the wider body. And there were times when he allowed the members to make important decisions because he wanted it to be more of an organization-wide decision.

4. He respected his members and always invited the use of the skills of the members. He felt that there was a task for every single individual member of the organization and that every member had a talent that could be used.

5. He earned the respect of the members. Many of us members joined the organization because we wanted something different from the 'politics as usual' and this new organization represented that. Our leader earned our respect because when the pundits would talk about him, and say that he wasn't enough of a 'politician' because he wasn't prepared to play the games of politics, we grew to respect him even more.

Observers of this organization would often express that

they didn't understand the loyalty of its members. They didn't understand our commitment to our leader even after defeat. They didn't understand why we worked so hard against all odds and with so little gain. Even I was once asked, "Why would you want to be a part of a party that could never win?" And my answer was, "My choice is not about winning or losing, it's about being a part of the solution." And even though we were never able to succeed, I don't regret any efforts I made, any time I spent, or any resources I commited to that cause. It wasn't just the organization and its cause that made me so commited, but its leader who, despite the odds, was commited to trying to bring about the change that was needed for the positive growth of a nation. And if I could, I would do it all over again.

This leader was an effective leader because he created a culture of partnership; he respected everybody's individual talents; he communicated with us on a continuous basis; he involved everyone in all of the decision making or created the perception of our influence in his decision making; he understood that all of us were connected in our common cause and had to work together to achieve the organizational goals; and he always praised members' performance when celebrating milestones. I don't know if this was his plan or intent, but his leadership style produced a cadre of workers that were totally committed to him as leader and who worked tirelessly for the cause. This is the kind of action from a leader that is congruent for this new consciousness model. Yes, he had faults, as we all do. However, his faults never diminished his leadership style because in our work, he always made it about us, and not himself. Now that's a leader!

Chapter 12: I Hear Your Actions

"Treat employees like partners, and they act like partners."

Fred Allen[15]

Who Are You Really?

Every act by management has meaning and communicates a message. Employees are in a continuous mode of interpretation and their perception of a message is always colored by their beliefs about executives and management.

All communications within an organization are perceived by employees to either be in their best interest or not in their best interest. It doesn't much matter what your intent is. As a popular saying goes, "The meaning of your communication is the response you get." If employees generally believe that executives respect them and have their best interest at heart, they will tend to perceive management's communications positively. On the other hand, if they believe that executives do not respect them or have their best interest at heart, they will tend to perceive communications negatively and can even view positive communications or positive behavior negatively.

15   *Quote Source: http://quotationsbook.com/quote/5060/*

I had a very surprising experience of this with a past client. I was brought into the organization as a consultant to help determine what the organizational challenges were. The level of distrust toward the top executive was so high among staff members that even though they were told that I was brought in to help address their challenges, they would not accept it. When I was introduced to a particular group of staff members bold enough to voice their opinion, they accused me of being brought in to tell management what management wanted to hear. They had been complaining for a long time about specific issues, yet the organizational climate was such that any individual brought in to listen to their issues and address them was met with complete skepticism and distrust.

So, with every act that I engaged in within that organization, I had to communicate a message of integrity, independence, fairness, openness, and a desire to truly help resolve staff issues. Here is an example of how the simplest act can communicate a message: When I conducted an organizational assessment, I had to be very careful of each step: Even though I communicated that the surveys were anonymous and did not require names (no space was provided for names), a few expressed that I could find a way to determine which survey belonged to whom. At the onset, they didn't trust the process. So when some individuals would attempt to hand their completed surveys to me instead of placing it in the box on the other side of the room, I would leave my seat, get the box, and present the box to them to place their survey within themselves, and then return the box to the other side of the room. I refused to touch any of the surveys individually. This was just one of the many steps taken to help build a sense of trust in the assessment process.

Interestingly enough, after building a level of trust among most of the staff, they did come to believe that I had their best interest at heart. However, they didn't change their views of management. In fact, each of the persons randomly chosen to be interviewed (as a part of my assessment) communicated that despite my efforts and results, they believed that management would not act on any of the information I provided. (This sentiment was always expressed unsolicited.) So, my individual actions to build trust worked for me, but did nothing to change the employees' distrust of management, despite my efforts to tie in the positive intervention with management's concern for them.

The act of continuous interpreting by employees does not stop at verbal or written messages directed toward employees. As previously mentioned, employees watch management's behavior with customers, suppliers and other stakeholders and these actions contribute to their overall view of management and executives. If they observe unethical behavior by the company, they come to believe that this is who company executives really are and view all else as just an act on the part of management.

Therefore, it is even more incumbent upon executives and managers to always communicate with intent and not by accident. While this may sound like an arduous task, it is not that difficult to do. It is not that employees are so delicate that they require kid glove treatment; it is simply that they wish to be treated with respect and as the powerful self-determining individuals that they are.

Respect is one of the most important values for individuals within and outside of the workplace. People want to always be respected no matter what their positions are within an organization. When management can imbue every communication with respect for employees, half of the battle of motivating employees is won.

One way in which respect is communicated is through employee participation, i.e. by soliciting their ideas and input, and while it may not always be practical, prudent, or desirous to do so, the perception of participation, partnership, and respect must always be maintained. There are several ways to do this.

A Partnership, Really?

First of all, you have to always create a sense of partnership. The perspective of partnership should guide all communications, whether it is written, verbal, or behavioral communications. And remember, every communication sends a message, so all messages need to be congruent, always. Saying one thing and doing another sends confusing messages. In such instances, employees will tend to believe what they see as opposed to what they hear.

When memos are sent out, they should always reflect an attitude of respect and appreciation. Employees should never be surprised by any information in a memo. If a memo is communicating a new procedure, this procedure should have been discussed and created with the participation of employees as would be reflected in a partnership. Remember, employee participation is a very important component of this model.

If an employee is a partner, they must be treated as a partner in every respect. Therefore, memos about poor performance and bad behavior should not be a policy. As previously mentioned, review sessions should be utilized and the challenges explored in a manner that still communicates 'I respect you.' In a situation where an individual continually exhibits such challenges, review sessions should be held more often, although given a different label, and efforts made to either assist the individual, if salvageable, or facilitate the ending of the partnership, if necessary. However, this must be done in a manner that is consistently conducive to the new consciousness approach as outlined in the chapter that follows.

Lend Me Your Ear

A simple tool that can be effectively utilized to help maintain a sense of participation, partnership, and respect is listening. When people are allowed to fully express themselves, they feel that the listener cares about what they have to say. This can cultivate a sense of participation, self-importance and respect in employees. Listening is important because executives are not always going to be in a position to allow employees to actually participate, although every effort should be made to do so. If management is cultivating a sense of participation through listening, it serves the purpose, which is to help employees feel like partners. However, know that listening isn't just about allowing someone to express him or herself. How one listens determines one's level of effectiveness.

Effective listening requires full engagement:

1. You must give your full attention to the individual speaking. This means full eye contact, body facing the individual, appropriate facial expressions (no bored looks), and no distracting movements like looking at your watch and watching people walk by. Even a child knows when you are not fully listening as I discovered when my daughter was four. She kept calling my name to get my attention. I answered her each time, but did not look up at her. She asked, "Are you listening?" And I answered, "Yes," still without looking up. Then she said, "No you are not Mommy. You are not looking at me." Naturally, this got my attention, and I realized that I couldn't even get away with this with a four-year-old.

2. You must acknowledge what the individual is saying. This can be done in two ways: If you wish to remain non-committal to any ideas being expressed, statements of "ahhs," and "umms," and head nodding communicates that you hear what they are saying. If you like and agree with what is being expressed, statements like "fantastic," "great idea," "awesome," and "interesting" communicates your feelings about

the idea. Both responses communicate that you are open and willing to listen to their ideas.

3. If you want to encourage sharing or participation, parrot back to the individual what you are hearing. This encourages the individual to keep talking and lets them know you are truly listening. Also, if you want to take the information away with you, summarize what you are hearing to ensure that you are clear on their ideas.

A little goes a long way. These simple tips can do a world of good in communicating respect, openness, and a willingness to have employee participation thus creating the culture of partnership that is the essence of this approach.

Cultivating Self-Leadership

Cultivating self-leadership is another way to maintain a sense of participation, partnership, and respect. Cultivating self-leadership in employees not only creates accountability, but also sends the message that 'we respect your ability to lead yourself,' and 'we view you as a partner.' The components of this model previously outlined suggest a structure that is based on self-leadership and partnership, but cultivating self-leadership can be taken a step further. You can cultivate self-leadership by building problem solving skills, such as the following example shows.

In a past job where I was in charge of several diverse departments, my Vice President lived thousands of miles away and only visited my location a few times a year. However, we communicated by telephone several times a week. I remember thinking that he was one of the best bosses I ever had because he lived thousands of miles away in a different time zone. But I later realized, at a time of reflection, that this sentiment had more to do with his management style than anything else.

I remember the first time I called him up with a major challenge very early in my employment with that company. After I explained the problem, he asked me a series of questions:

1. What created the problem?
2. What impact is it having?
3. What are you doing to fix it?
4. What are you doing to avoid it from happening in the future?

After I answered his questions, he said "okay," and moved to the next topic. I was floored by his response. Never before did I have an experience where 'the boss' did not want to take control in a work situation. From that day forward, I worked extra hard to analyze any difficult situations to impress him on my handling of all unexpected challenges. I always did a full analysis of the situation before calling him and discovered that the head office would often follow my suggestions (when it involved them) as a result of it.

I then found myself following the lead of my VP. I taught my staff how to conduct assessments of challenging situations for themselves. I would often talk to them about our business philosophy and our basic objectives with customers. I figured that if they understood what was important, then they could make decisions for themselves in problem situations.

Another part of the reason I did this was because I did not have the time to always run and solve the problems for each of my departments. What I discovered was that members of one department in particular would resolve their challenges and then call me up to explain what they did, and why they did it. And they would actually say that their choice of resolutions was based on how they perceived I would have resolved it given the philosophy I always espoused. And they were usually on target.

So, not only did this approach work with me as an employee,

as a manager it worked with my employees as well. There are several reasons for this. First of all, the entire company was on a first name basis, including the President of the company. This automatically engendered a feeling of equality. Secondly, looking to employees to resolve challenges involves them, and communicates respect and a sense of trust in their abilities. The lack of micromanaging communicates trust and a sense of partnership.

I would give employees work objectives and allow them to manage their time, and they would work hard to deliver good results. While I may have had other employee challenges, I never had any 'slackers.' They all seemed to want to deliver results, and being left on their own to self-lead worked. Interestingly enough, the only complaint I ever got from one or two of my departments is that they didn't see me often enough. Can you imagine that—wanting to see 'the boss' more often and not less? This is what self-leadership can do.

I eventually realized that the real reason I liked my boss was because he trusted me, treated me with respect, allowed me to participate in management in an independent and meaningful way, and viewed me as a partner in the organization's efforts to achieve its objectives. He was truly a leader and not a 'boss.'

People like to be trusted and seen as responsible and this is seen even in children. Think about how often you experienced kids insisting on doing something on their own, begging to be trusted to take responsibility for things. Then they work hard to prove themselves. Well, this need for independence and a sense of responsibility does not go away in adulthood. Adults want that same sense of independence and trust from their leaders. Using the tool of self-leadership can go a long way to teach problem-solving skills, and to communicate a sense of participation, partnership, and respect.

It would be rather challenging to discuss all of the aspects of organizational life that create opportunities to communicate the right messages and communicate respect. Nevertheless, always asking yourself, "how can I communicate respect and a sense of partnership?" will keep you headed on the right path. And when the opportunities to consistently communicate the right messages do appear you will be ready. Always remember though, actions speak louder than words.

Chapter 13: But, But, But...

"...we do not prune dead trees to make them fruitful, nor those which are planted in a desert; but such as belong to the garden, and possess life."

Arrowsmith[16]

Having read this far, you might be thinking, "In a perfect world maybe this could work, but..." Despite your concerns, which may certainly be valid, there is no doubt that this approach can help you achieve your goals. However, this approach will not work with every employee. It is not due to the approach, but due to the fact that some employees have made choices for themselves that no matter what the business structure may be, they are not the right fit.

RELEASE INCONGRUENT INDIVIDUALS

These individuals are the ones that do not wish to be working within the organization in the first place. They are the ones who have internal issues that would stand in the way of the work performance no matter what tools and support they are

16   *Quote Source: http://www.giga-usa.com/quotes/topics/resignation_ t001.htm*

given. And they are the ones that can have an energetically negative impact on your organizational progress.

One thing many of us recognize about life is that each individual has to make his or her own decisions about their actions and their future. Many have proven that no matter how much you may try to help or support individuals, you cannot change their behavior or choices if they don't want to. These individuals must be allowed the freedom to live their own lives and choices, but not within your organization. Therefore, it will be necessary to release individuals that are not the right fit for your organization.

However, the approach to the separation process is just as important as the components previously outlined. Remember, your communication must always be in alignment with the philosophy of 'you are just as important as I am; your goals are just as important as mine.' You can take this position and still do what is in the company's best interest. It's really about not having any judgment about the individual's choice, yet acknowledging that his or her employment within your company is not in the company's best interest, and then communicating honestly to the individual that he or she is not the right fit.

While this communicates good will to the individual being terminated, it is just as important for the employees who remain. Employees watch every action of management and executives, and form opinions based on actions that they see and not on what they are told. If in any action you show a lack of concern for any individual, employees come to believe that that is who you truly are and not the 'gazillion' good actions you may have demonstrated in the past. Since this model is based on the premise that employees are just as important to the organization as its executives, it is imperative that this point is not taken lightly and that care is taken when terminating employees.

Some may feel that this is difficult to do. And while I could only give specific suggestions based on each company's situation, I can relate an experience I had to demonstrate this position. While working for a large chain, I was asked to lay off nine individuals from a particular department, with good reason I might add. However, despite the validity of the decision, we were located in a jurisdiction that had very strict labor laws. The government required companies to receive government approvals prior to any lay offs. The alternative was getting the employees to agree to be terminated.

So my challenge became to get nine people to agree to end their employment. The first thing I had to do was come up with a convincing argument as to why this was in their best interest—remember, individuals act in their own best interest—and at the end of the day I did. I strategized on the order of the meetings that I needed to have with each of them to prevent any undue influence on each other; I saw two best friends at the same time so I could watch and control how they influenced each other; and I saw the two most difficult employees last (separately) hoping that everyone else had left the property and they would not have access to the others once they learned their own fate. The result: Seven initially agreed to accept the termination and final pay, and two didn't—naturally the two I met with last. While the process following the initial meetings got difficult and complicated (because the two dissenters contacted the others and convinced them to file a complaint with the Labor Department), in the end they all eventually accepted the payout and termination without the company requiring Labor Department approval.

There were several reasons why this worked—albeit a circuitous route to the final result. At the core was the approach that was taken. I had decided that I needed to 'make it about them'—in a good way. I didn't tell them the department was being downsized because "you were ineffective, corrupt, and we have evidence of underhanded dealings," although all of this was true. My goal was to get them to agree to the termination so there would not be a long drawn out fight at the Department of Labor. It was not about 'pay back'; it was about achieving the goal.

I focused on communicating that 'the company cared about them' and wanted what was in their best interest, which it was not able to deliver on any more. The action that made this appear as sincere and not just espoused was the additional payout given beyond what was required by law. Yes, this did cost the company some additional money, but not half as much as it would have cost if the matter went before the Labor Department and attorney fees were involved.

My point is as stated before. People are human beings. They want to be respected, appreciated, and considered important. You are far more likely to get cooperation of whatever kind is necessary whenever you treat individuals from this perspective.

It is very important to note however, that there is a distinct difference between an employee with no ambition and an employee with no desire to be productive. Low ambition does not equate to low performance or lack of motivation. That is why it is key to ensure that each employee has the necessary tools and support, and is given every opportunity to succeed at their job function. Not every poor performance is reflective of the individual's lack of desire to be productive. Each case of poor performance must be assessed individually to determine its cause.

It may not easily become clear to you what the challenges are, so it is necessary to assess all of the components related to the job function. If you have the distinct impression that a particular worker is a good worker, but is demonstrating low performance, check out the systems, processes, and structure. If the problem is not in any of these components, review the individual's skill set and knowledge base. Also, ensure that the individual is not a square peg being forced into a round hole. If this is not the challenge, then it must be a motivation issue. If the company is doing its part to motivate individuals—as outlined in this model—then the challenge is internal. It could be personality conflicts at work that are negatively impacting the individual, or it could be challenges outside of work that are affecting job performance.

While it is a wise company policy to not become involved in the personal lives of employees, providing a listening ear can go a long way in improving the state of mind of individuals with challenges, even though you are not resolving their challenges. Being able to express oneself and 'get it off your chest' is helpful in moving past challenges. So listening can be helpful. Nevertheless, it is expected that these are occasional challenges that one is lending support for and not challenges that are having long term affect on work performance.

The bottom line is to be clear on which employees can fit into this model where both the company and the individual can be partners and benefit; and also be clear on which employees cannot assist your organization and vice versa—always without judgment.

Chapter 14: Le Résistance

"We don't have to remain in this radically destructive mind-set and institutional-set. We can change, and the natural order of things could emerge in all of our societal organizations— government, commerce, religion—it's right there, waiting to happen. I often tell people that every mind is like a room in an old house, stuffed with very old furniture. Take any space in your mind and empty it of your old conceptions and new ones will rush in, good or bad. So change is more a getting rid of rather than an adding to or an acquiring."

Dee Hock [17]

If you are seriously interested in implementing this approach, you have to begin by changing your wineskins. Remember, new wine in old wineskins will not work. You have to begin with a new mindset.

In order to view your employees as equal to yourself, you have to review your sense of self. Many individuals derive their value and sense of self from what they do—their profession. We are many things. However, our value as human beings should not be based on our roles in life or our professions. We are each

17 *Quote Source: WIE: Business Transformation Through Chaos Theory: http://www.wie.org/j22/hock.asp*

valuable as individual human beings; we simply make different choices about how we express ourselves and how we employ our talents and skills in the world.

I am not suggesting that one cannot feel proud of and excited by one's professional attainment and accomplishments. Of course one can. What I am suggesting is that if our value of ourselves is based on our professional titles, it engenders a certain attitude and specific behaviors toward others, which may not allow us to facilitate the growth and development of others, thus preventing outstanding achievements with bottom-line results.

Having your identity and sense of self-rooted in being a manager, for example, means you view this as your value. If your role of being in charge or responsible for people was to change, then your value of yourself would change. Investing one's identity in one's professional title is what causes some of the internal challenges, such as depression, that some executives face when their roles ultimately change.

To effectively adopt this new consciousness model, your view of yourself would have to change because your role would have to change. You would have to go from being a 'boss' to becoming a leader, and from being a 'manager' to becoming a facilitator. A facilitator in this context is one that would facilitate the growth and development of employees. The facilitator's purpose would be to help those employees be the best that they can be in achieving the company's goals, as well as to help employees achieve their individual goals, which could include becoming a manager—facilitator—as well one day. This employee goal may intimidate an individual with a manager mindset.

Letting Go Of Control

In addition to becoming a facilitator, you would have to give up control. Giving up control does not mean accepting chaos;

it means giving up individual control and a micro management style in order to lead others to become self-leaders. It is a matter of choosing a different method of operational control. It's a transfer of power from 'boss control' to 'employee self-control.' This allows for less stress on your part, more accountability on their part, and everyone working toward the same goal as a matter of choice as opposed to a matter of coercion.

Keep in mind, however, that not every employee may be excited by an opportunity to be a self-leader, even if they are competent. Some lack self-confidence and don't wish the responsibility, so this cultivation may have to happen over a period of time with some employees moving towards independence faster than others. The timing of this is crucial because you want to avoid overwhelming your employees and having them lose confidence in themselves if they are not succeeding.

If you are choosing to adopt this model and its approach for your business, you have to trust in the process on all fronts. Achieving the objectives is not just a result of the operational structure. The way employees perceive their place within the organization is a very influential factor in their level of motivation and productivity. All aspects of this model work together to create organizational effectiveness, increased productivity, an improved bottom line, and fulfilled employees.

Chapter 15: Ready, Set, Go!

"I am only one, but I am one. I cannot do everything, but I can do something. And I will not let what I cannot do interfere with what I can do."

Edward Everett Hale (1822-1909)[18]
American author and Unitarian minister

Aren't you tired of the ineffective ways businesses operate? What about the inability of your organization to maximize its potential? Don't you think there is a connection between the general malaise of most employees in the work place and business structures and performance? Are you prepared to be bold and try something drastically new?

Even at its onset, such an approach as this yields benefits to the organization. There are several reasons why such a model makes sense: It increases the likelihood that organizational targets will be achieved because individual objectives and targets are set as a part of the overall goals and objectives of the organization; it steers employees directly toward company goals; it cultivates a continued focus on organizational targets

---

18   *Quote Source:http://thinkexist.com/quotation/i_am_only_one-but_i_am_one-i_can-t_do_everything/205060.html*

and objectives; and it increases the likelihood of organizational success.

Involving employees in organizational planning and strategizing gives them a sense of ownership. We all know that human beings take much better care of those things that belong to them as opposed to things that do not. Furthermore, people protect that in which they feel a sense of ownership. They become protective to the point of policing each other to ensure that everyone's behavior is in keeping with where the organization is trying to go. With each employee's work role and work tasks directly aligned with the overall objectives, employees are directly working toward achievement of the organization's strategic goals.

Changing to the new consciousness model does require some flexibility. It does require some effort and time. It does require movement of people and a shift in how things are done and time for it all to settle in. Actually, in most cases it requires a major overhaul in thinking and action. However, the alternative is to have the same failed efforts to get employees motivated to work toward your company goals, the same failed strategies that fail because they happen in isolation of each other, and subsequently the same lack-luster performance results. But imagine if you were able to get most of your people in the right positions, working towards company objectives and hitting targets that really set your company on a path of record performance. Imagine employee accountability. Imagine record bottom-line performance. Wouldn't it be worth it all?

Incorporating this philosophical approach into your organization will result in employees who are more accountable, and more individually motivated. This approach gives executives the capacity to utilize bottom-line measures to assess individual, departmental and organizational progress. This also allows managers to spend less time micro-managing employees and more time on managing operations.

However, remember the first core requirement for

implementing this approach: You have to view each employee as just as important as yourself, and his or her goals as just as important as your goals. Unless you can do this, do not bother trying to implement this model. It will fail!

The act of 'being human' in the workplace is always occurring beneath the surface. It impacts and is impacted by every aspect of organizational life. It is these behavioral dynamics that influence employee motivation and productivity. While many executives would like to ignore any human behavior dynamics and simply focus on achieving organizational goals, using human behavior dynamics to your advantage can maximize output and tremendously increase bottom line results. However, executives need always keep in mind that organizational and behavioral dynamics are always in motion, and pseudo adoption of this approach will not yield the desired results. It must be widespread and adopted by all of management. There must be consistency in the use of this approach, otherwise you defeat the purpose of engaging at all.

The one thing that I want to point out about this approach is that several of the aspects mentioned are not new to business. It incorporates existing business approaches—a knitting together of sorts. All it takes is the courage to be progressive, to engage in true 'out of the box' thinking and behaving, and to use logic to go about getting what you really want from employees instead of 'doing things the way they have always been done.'

This model presents an opportunity for effective leadership on many levels. The new role becomes one of leading rather than commanding or ordering. Real leaders understand that it is not about 'bossing people around,' but rather serving people. It's about being a facilitator, not a boss. Ultimately, it's about transforming your organizational dynamics and achieving unprecedented performance results.

The aim of this model is to provide the tools for implementing practical Psychology in a business setting. It takes human behavior principles and uses them to guarantee the achievement of bottom line results. It is essential that any pseudo adoption of this model be avoided, as it can cause more harm than good. The depth of this concept needs to be fully understood and then, if chosen, its adoption needs to become embedded within the organization in order for its value to be fully realized. All the best in your quest for

*A New Consciousness,
A Different Path,
A New Approach,
A Different Result!*

About the Author

Cathy Archer has worked in the field of Organization Development for the past ten years. Having a Bachelor of Arts degree in Psychology and a Master of Science degree in Human Resources Development, she focused her consulting practice on organizational assessments. This led to her being called into a number of organizations to study employee morale challenges. She found similar themes that resulted in challenges throughout a number of the organizations she assessed, and feels that many of the challenges that executives face can be avoided. As a result, she formulated a new consciousness model that she feels work best in helping executives achieve their business goals through a more effective functioning of the organization. Her new consciousness model meets the needs of executives for bottom-line results, while meeting the needs of employees for independence and fulfillment at work.

In her desire to help individuals over the years, Cathy Archer created and hosted a radio show entitled, "Success is Yours," and published a weekly newspaper column entitled, "Performance Challenges? Ask Cathy". These projects were designed to help businesses with human resources challenges and overall business development. She is now focusing all of her energies on coaching and writing. In her coaching sessions she guides her clients through her new consciousness approach, offers practical tips, and answers questions for implementing this model within their organizations. (For information on coaching services using Cathy Archer's New Consciousness Model go to www.ADifferentPath.info) She also has plans to publish more books in the 'A Different Path' series.

Cathy approaches life from a metaphysical perspective, which colors everything that she does. The approach outlined in her book is steeped in a New Consciousness Philosophy.

She believes that our philosophy of life cannot be packed away when it is not a convenient fit for the various aspects of our lives; instead, we should strive to always reinvent the way we live, if necessary, to reflect our personal philosophy in each aspect of our lives. She is committed to always seeking ways to have her life reflect her personal philosophy.

Cathy is a part of a group called The Crimson Circle, which meets online monthly to discuss a New Consciousness approach to life. These group discussions have inspired her writings. She lives in both The Bahamas and Florida with her daughter Cristin, and she likes to spend her time writing. More information on her projects can be found at www.AdifferentPath.info